KU-102-561

LITERACY: TEXT AND CONTEXT

UNITED KINGDOM READING ASSOCIATION

Literacy:
Text and Context

Edited by
David Wray

Literacy: Text and Context

Editor: David Wray

ISBN: 1 897638 01 9

Published by: United Kingdom Reading Association
°/₀ Warrington Road County Primary School, Naylor Road, Widnes, Cheshire WA8 0BP, England.

© United Kingdom Reading Association,
July 1993

British Library Catalogue in Publication. A catalogue record for this book is available from the British Library

Contents

Literacy: Text and Context

David Wray

Introduction: text and context

A group of teacher trainees were asked to write about their memories of their own first encounters with reading and writing. The following accounts were typical:

"I don't remember much about reading in the infants school. I think we used Peter and Jane. I remember getting very excited when I brought my first book home from the library. It was the story of Peter Rabbit and my mum had already read it to me at home. I insisted on reading it to Mum, Dad and my older brother that night before I would go to bed. I've still got a copy of that book, although the original fell apart through being read so much."

"I wrote a book when I was six. It was all about dinosaurs. We had been watching a television series at school and after each programme we had to copy out some notes from the blackboard. I decided to write about the programmes in my own words at home. My mother still has the book although it's a bit dog-eared now."

What these students seemed to remember were two inter-related aspects of their experience of learning to read and write. First and foremost they remembered particular texts which they read or wrote. Asking a group of junior school children to do a similar activity produced an even greater emphasis upon texts. They talked about books, comics, magazines and, in one case, cereal packets. Such anecdotal evidence of the influence of texts upon literate and proto-literate people fits with an increased recent emphasis upon the importance of text itself in the development of literacy. Until fairly recently, somewhat surprisingly, text, the essential material of literacy, has been rather neglected in research into and developments in literacy teaching.

The other aspect which featured largely in the accounts of both students and children was the range of contexts in which they had experienced reading and writing. They talked mainly about collaborative contexts, positively about those involving a parent or a sibling in which the shared enterprise of literacy was important, and, disturbingly, almost universally negatively about the classroom contexts in which they had been required to struggle with the performance of reading and writing.

It seems that text and context represent two crucial dimensions to the acquisition and development of literacy and it behoves us to try to understand them better.

Elsewhere (Wray, 1992) I have outlined and discussed a model for literacy development which brings together these two dimensions and attempts to use the concept of authorship (in the sense of the creation and recreation of meaning) to resolve certain apparent conflicts in attention to aspects of the model. This model tries to suggest that the 'traditional' view of teaching (according to which the teacher possesses knowledge and skills which he/she attempts to transmit to the children) is entirely inadequate to describe our current extensive knowledge about the processes of literacy acquisition. Such view ignores the crucial influence upon these processes of the contexts in which learning takes place and of the texts which are read and written in the process of the learning.

Of these dimensions there has, perhaps, been greatest emphasis recently upon context, in the sense of an environment for learning. Stress has been placed upon the need for teachers to provide demonstrations of literacy, to create atmospheres in which children feel safe to learn through experimentation and in which they get regular practice of using literacy for real purposes, and to structure carefully the support children are offered ('scaffolding' in Bruner's terms) as they 'emerge into literacy'. Such has been the power of these ideas that it has sometimes seemed that teachers have been advised that all they need to do is create a suitable context and children will just learn. The reality is, of course, that the business of teaching is not so simple and it is likely that a suitable classroom context is a necessary but not sufficient condition for the efficient learning of literacy.

Attention has also been given to the wider contexts of literacy learning, both social and political, and it is now common to read discussions about the influence upon literacy development of particular social contexts, such as the family, and about the place of critical literacy in macro and micro-political social developments.

The dimension of text has been much more neglected in work on literacy yet it is at the very centre of the learning process. Children read and write texts, teachers teach reading and writing with and through texts, and texts provide a context for understanding, creating and responding to themselves and other texts. Modern literary theory lays great stress upon the idea that texts are never autonomous entities but are rather 'intertextual constructs: sequences which have meaning in relation to other texts which they take up, cite, parody, refute, or generally transform'. (Culler, 1981, p.38) It would be possible to conceive of literacy development as being simply a matter of a progressive elaboration of textual and intertextual experience.

Attention to the nature and importance of text has come from two quite distinct directions of interest, which have at times seemed contradictory in their implications. One of these directions might be termed the structuralist approach as it has involved the close analysis of the structure of texts, from a linguistic perspective largely inspired by the work of Halliday. Drawing upon the Hallidayan analysis of language as social semiotic (Halliday, 1978), the group of Australian researchers collectively known as 'genre theorists' have looked closely at the ways in which text structures reflect a variety of social ways of making meaning (Halliday & Hasan, 1989). The implication of this work is that, unless some attention is actually given to teaching children to operate effectively within the genre structures upon which society is based, children are, in fact, disenfranchised from large parts of wider social life (Christie, 1990).

The second direction from which interest in text has come might be termed the authenticist approach, as it has emphasised the importance of 'real' texts, that is, texts written for authentic purposes (as opposed to mere instructional purposes such as reading scheme texts). Several notable educationalists (for example, Meek, 1988) have pointed out the ways in which authentic texts can teach readers many important lessons about reading and one of the major motivations underlying what has been termed in Britain the 'real books movement' (very closely linked with the whole language movement in the United States) has been the superiority of authentic texts to linguistically controlled scheme texts. In writing, similarly, authenticity has loomed large. The process writing approach, inspired by the work of Graves (1983), has placed great emphasis upon children 'finding their own voices' and composing texts which have real importance to them.

The structuralist and authenticist ways of looking at text have sometimes seemed to be in opposition to each other. Structuralist views have been caricatured as implying a return to the dry, direct teaching of textual features, reviving suspicions about the effectiveness and lack of child-centredness of grammar exercises. Authenticist approaches, on the other hand, have been caricatured as being structureless and giving no attention at all to developing children's awareness of textual conventions. Both these criticisms rest, of course, upon misunderstandings and the two positions do seem potentially to have much in common. In essence they are both concerned with children's responses to and production of 'real' texts. The genre theorists have continually emphasised that textual structures, and thus the teaching of them, only make sense within a context of meaning. Both positions, therefore, emphasise purpose and meaning in literacy development.

They are both also concerned with increasing children's control over their reception and production of texts and, as such, have an important implication for ideas of appropriate contexts for literacy learning. For 'real books' and process-writing advocates the issue of children's choice is in the foreground of their intentions. Only by being allowed to make choices about what they read and write, they argue, can children develop the personal investment in the processes of literacy which is essential if they are to engage in real learning of these processes. For structuralists, developing children's control over the ways in which text is used for particular purposes in society is one of the foundations of their arguments. 'To learn to recognise and create the various genres found in one's culture is to learn to exercise choices - choices in building and ordering different kinds of meaning and hence, potentially, choices in directing the course of one's life' (Christie, 1990, p.3).

The papers in this volume

The papers collected here all contribute in their various ways to our understandings of these and other crucial issues to do with the nature and role of text and context in literacy learning.

The book is divided into two sections, the first of which contains papers centred around the theme of text and the second around that of context. It will quickly be apparent to the reader that, such is the inter-relatedness of these two dimensions, each paper in fact could probably equally well have been placed in the other section! This is natural, as any text can itself be seen as a context for the use of literacy and any context, to the extent to which it becomes amenable to analysis and comment, becomes itself a text.

The book begins with two papers, from Jeff Hynds and David Lewis, which discuss, each from their own standpoint, the neglected importance of the texts from which children learn to read. Attention then moves to a consideration of children's knowledge about texts. Bob Leather and Tony Martin describe their studies of different types of text use and Alison Littlefair discusses the importance of knowledge about genre and register. Pamela Owen outlines her research into children's use of textual knowledge in writing and Joyce Morris presents a critical analysis of the texts used for statutory assessment purposes. Three papers then follow focusing on non-fiction text and children's learning from it. Joseph Rivard discusses the teaching of text structure in both electronic and print environments, while Sara Brody looks critically at ways of helping students link what they read with what they already know. Marion Tonjes gives some further, practical ideas for teaching with texts.

Section 2 of the book begins with two papers which set a social context for literacy teaching. John Aldridge discusses the links which are possible between school and the world outside through the use of newspapers and Keith Nettle outlines the current 'state' of reading and the printed word. Both of these contributors work outside the world of schools and classrooms but in areas crucially dependent upon literacy. Their observations are, therefore, especially fresh and welcome.

The five papers which follow take us firmly back into the classroom as they each present different perspectives on the contexts for literacy provided therein. Ros Fisher discusses the role of the teacher in enabling early literacy learning specifically in terms of the creation and maintenance of contexts for learning. Rebecca Huss describes her research into the classroom contexts for learning created by and for children learning English as a second language in schools in England. Loreta Stewart outlines the beneficial effects upon children's writing of a more purposeful classroom context, an observation very similar to the kind which stimulated Jane Medwell to undertake her research into classroom contexts for writing. Medwell in fact argues that the picture is more complex and she discusses several possible interpretations of what she found. Finally here Juliet Partridge outlines the contribution to a language learning context of language awareness developed through play activities.

One educational context which few people can escape nowadays is that of the demand for ever more thorough assessment of children's progress. Christine Leland discusses several approaches to this, while Louise Poulson describes the ways in which teachers in one part of England were observed to be handling the issue of assessment. The next two papers both look in different ways at the context provided by children's home backgrounds. Julie Spreadbury examines the ways in which parents interacted with their children during story sharing time and Jo Weinberger looks at the place of literacy and literate activities in the home contexts of young children.

The final three papers bring our view outwards again as they each make reference to the political context of literacy development. Margaret Cook and Sylvia Karavis outline the contribution to an understanding of reading made by the LINC project materials - materials which, for political reasons, lost the support of the British Government only days before they were due to be published (and now may never be). Katharine Davies Samway and Lucinda Pease-Alvarez present their survey of the views of teachers describing themselves as 'whole language teachers', a term which in itself has become political. Roger Beard concludes the book by presenting his arguments in favour of a balanced approach to literacy. The issue of teaching methods (and, indeed, the very definition of literacy) is, and has always been, a political one in all countries of the world.

Readers will assuredly agree that the chapters in this book cover a vast range of topics and issues and this brief introduction can in no way do them justice. I hope that they will be read eagerly and with profit and, above all, that they make a lively and worthwhile contribution to the at times fierce but always marvellously stimulating debates about literacy, about texts and about contexts.

References

CHRISTIE, F. (1990). The changing face of literacy. In Christie, F. (Ed.) *Literacy for a Changing World* (pp. 1-25). Hawthorn, Victoria: Australian Council for Educational Research.

CULLER, J. (1981). *The Pursuit of Signs*. London: Routledge & Kegan Paul.

GRAVES, D. (1983). *Writing: Teachers and Children at Work*. Portsmouth, New Hampshire: Heinemann.

HALLIDAY, M. & HASAN, R. (1989). *Language, Context and Text*. Oxford: Oxford University Press.

HALLIDAY, M. (1978). *Language as Social Semiotic*. London: Edward Arnold.

MEEK, M. (1988). *How Texts Teach What Readers Learn*. Stroud: Signal Press.

WRAY, D. (1992) 'Literacy: bringing back the text' in Satow, F. & Gatherer, W. (eds) *Literacy without Frontiers* Widnes: United Kingdom Reading Association

Text and Neglect

Jeff Hynds

The crucial role played by certain kinds of books and texts in learning to read and write has, on the whole, been very little considered by literacy experts or indeed by many teachers. Even books about the teaching of reading published recently by celebrated people are quite likely to give little serious attention to the nature of the texts that children are provided with in school, and the consequent effects upon their learning. Some make no mention of books or texts at all. It is as if they feel that it does not matter what you learn to read with, as long as you learn to read. But in this paper I want to suggest that it is what you habitually read (or have read to you) that decides what kind of reader you become. What you read determines not only how you read, but whether you read, and even whether you can. I also equally believe that what you habitually read determines how you write, but I shall not have time, in the space of a short paper, to develop this further.

This is not to say that the texts that are used for the teaching of reading in school have never been considered at all. As *The Reading Book* says, "People have never thought that texts did not matter in the teaching of reading. In the past, many debates about reading have in fact centred around the texts". (Barrs & Thomas, 1991, p.56).

But in fact these were special texts that had been deliberately created to reflect particular theories of how reading is learnt. These theories were not only explained in the various handbooks accompanying the reading schemes to which the texts belonged, but were, as *The Reading Book* observes, "apparent from the very nature of the texts themselves" (p.56). The debates came about because the theories themselves were seen to be in conflict.

So what we had was a situation where conflicting theories of reading created special texts to be read. Now this seems to me to be the wrong way round. We want to be able to read the texts we already have, those that surround us and have been part of our lives for centuries. Equally we want to be able to read the texts that continue to be written in abundance every day (or some of them at least). If we are to have theories of reading then these theories must explain what we have to do with the texts we've already got. It is surely illogical to create special texts to fit theories, which in any case differ, and which might be false. (Since they differ, some presumably would be.) True theories of reading must be created to fit the texts we already have and know about and read. In reading, theories do not create texts; texts create theories. The texts came first, after all; how to read them must follow.

I could perhaps say at this point that I do not know of any scientific enterprise where, armed with a theory, people have gone out and constructed special evidence to base the theory on, all the while ignoring the actual evidence on which it should be based. Reading must be the only one!

Now none of this might have mattered if it had been some passing fashion, happening many years ago, but the fact is we still have this situation. These texts, specially created to fit theories, are endemic in our schools even now in 1992, and what is more they are the principal resource for the teaching of reading (and heavily influence writing). According to the most recent research, they are used by 83% of Year 2 teachers (Cato *et al* 1992, p.23).

My contention, in this paper, and in the course of my INSET work with teachers nationally, is that these theories are on the whole mistaken, and the texts created from them are false. They are untrue to what texts in the real world are like and to what normal reading involves. These theories and these texts, in short, ignore the actual reading behaviour of ordinary people, both children and adults, in the actual world in which we live.

Over the years a number of bodies of international research and theoretical investigation have, I believe, shown this to be so. I would like here to refer to two of these in particular. These researches are not all that new. Indeed, it would be possible to claim that in some respects they are at least 2,000 years old! You would think that by now they would be common knowledge. But in fact they have, for the most part, not been taken much notice of, or been ignored altogether, or simply not been understood. I have sometimes wondered whether or not they have been deliberately misunderstood, since to understand them would be to destroy too many entrenched beliefs!

These researches are based, firstly, on the actual behaviour of readers reading already existent books and texts in normal circumstances and, secondly, on the very nature, or the inner workings of, the texts themselves. I will consider them briefly now.

1. "Process" research

This body of research, which for convenience I will refer to as "process" research, is about what is actually happening when people read. It has been described and discussed in one way or another in many books, for example in Weaver (1988) or Clay (1991). What this research reveals is that reading, like other forms of language use (listening, spelling) is a <u>multi-cued</u> process; indeed <u>has</u> to be a multi-cued process or it does not happen.

One way of explaining this is as follows. In reading, although the actual print (the letters, the sounds, the sight words and so forth) does provide us with some information when we read, it does not provide us with anything like enough. If the print was all we had to go on we'd never be able to read. The fact is that when we read we have to get information from a number of sources, and some of these are in our brain already and not in the print before us. We have, or need to have, information systems in our heads, called "cue systems" which we have to use in order to read. Knowing how to use the cue systems is the most basic of all the basic skills of reading. There are at least four major cue systems, and each of these has at least two sub-divisions. At its simplest the reading process will look something like this:

CUE SYSTEMS IN THE READING PROCESS	
1. SYNTACTIC Knowledge of our own language	(a) We draw on the spoken language we already know to try to predict what words or phrases are coming and to confirm what we read. (b) We draw on our experience of "book" language to try to predict what words and phrases are coming and to confirm what we read.
2. SEMANTIC Expectation of what makes sense	(a) We use our general expectation of what makes sense in life to try to predict what's coming and to interpret what's happening. (b) We use the immediate textual context, especially previous context, to help work out the meaning and confirm what we read.
3. BIBLIOGRAPHIC Knowledge of how books and written texts work	(a) We use our knowledge of written genres, and how each functions, to help predict patters of possibility and confirm our interpretations. (b) We use our knowledge of the various conventions and arrangements of books and written texts as a guide to, and confirmation of, the intended meaning.
4. GRAPHOPHONIC Confirming and checking system using sight words and letter sounds	(a) We help the process along by recognising familiar words and phrases here and there, especially when these are content words and phrases learnt by the experience of reading. (b) We occasionally take note of, or check, letter-sound associations, especially if a doubt arises.

Optimum reading, even of an ordinary functional kind, requires the full and simultaneous operation of all these systems. If one isn't operating, then reading is more difficult, though you can usually get by for a short time. But if, for some reason, two or three are not functioning, then reading will become impossible. What is more, the order of the cue-systems is significant in that readers cannot develop the later systems before the earlier ones have been established and are operating. In order words, they have a progressively interdependent relationship.

This view of reading as a multi-cued process has many implications for the teaching of reading which lack of space will prevent me from discussing in any detail here. One or two examples must suffice. For a start, it will be obvious that to teach children to use only one, or even two, of the sub-systems will not help them very much. Over concentration on a so-called "method", like "look-and-say" or "phonics" will distort reading for children if they have not also learned to cue syntactically, semantically and bibliographically. Indeed I have found children who "know all their words" and are very good at "phonics", but who still struggle desperately when confronted with an actual text. They can read the word lists but not the texts! It's obvious why. What they know, however well they know it, is not enough, because, in reading, the print alone is not enough. And the danger is that they will come to depend on sight words and phonics and go on struggling for years. What process research tells us is that children who cannot read cannot, for some reason, draw on all their cue-systems. They do not know how to, or have no experience of doing it, or too little experience of doing it, or of seeing it done. If they knew how to draw on all their cue-systems they'd be able to read. So such children need to be taught how to draw on them. They don't need more phonics or sight words.

This of course is not to say (and there is particular misunderstanding here) that teachers don't have to teach phonics and sight words. Obviously they do, because the graphophonic cue-system is as vital as the other systems. But as it is fourth in line (so to speak), it has to be taught after the other three cue systems have begun to operate and in ways that allow it to combine with them. It will not make any sense on its own. To teach reading we have to help children to develop all their cue systems in the right order. Unfortunately, I will not have the opportunity in this short paper to discuss the various ways in which this can be done.

However, this is not all, by any means. If we want children not just to be able to read but to become truly literate, that is to become, as they grow older, really accomplished and expert readers, then we must pay attention to another very significant body of international research.

2. "Text" research

This research, which involves investigation into the nature of written texts, particularly as applied to the many thousands of outstanding books that are published for children nowadays, derives ultimately from developments in modern literary theory. This research has on the whole not been thought to have very much connection with the teaching of reading and writing. It is rarely mentioned by reading experts or psycholinguists. For example, a recently published and, in some quarters, much praised book by Adams (1990), described by the publishers as "the most complete review, within a single cover, of our expanding knowledge of the processes involved in learning to read", does not in fact give any serious attention to what is to be read by those doing the learning. (Nor, come to think of it, does it investigate reading as a multi-cued process, so it is by no means as "complete" as the publishers claim.) Even on teacher training courses it is apparently rare for the texts of children's books to be considered in any depth, according to some recent research (Brooks *et al* 1992, p.58).

As I suggested at the beginning of this paper, it seems to be quite commonly believed that almost anything will do to teach children to read as long as it "works". Text research, however, shows that books and texts vary enormously in the demands that they make on readers, and that this can crucially affect the way children read. (See, for example, Meek 1988, Styles *et al* 1992, Martin 1989, Chap.4).

Most of the normal texts of our world - for example stories, poetry, biography, newspapers - can be seen, on close inspection, to carry, in addition to the intended meaning, extra and other meanings, which may be strong and obvious or quite subtle. Some texts may even carry whole networks of meaning that are quite difficult to work out. Although this is more likely to happen in fiction (and particularly in poetry), it also happens quite frequently in non-fiction. The recent research reports on the teaching of reading, which I have already mentioned, would I'm sure be generally regarded as "objective" (Brooks *et al* 1992, Cato *et al* 1992). But to anyone "tuned in" to reports of this kind certain other meanings begin to appear. For example, the "objective" researchers reveal as much about themselves as they do about those they are investigating! In this case, the extra layers of meaning are presumably unintentional, but sometimes in reading it is difficult to tell what is intentional and what is not. Moreover, different readers may, at different times, apprehend meanings differently, and may contribute more meanings of their own. Good readers get used to this from their earliest days. Good readers always read more than what is there, whether they know they are doing it or not.

Reading, in other words, is a multivalent activity, because texts are multivalent. Reading is thus multi-cued in process and multivalent in effect. If children don't read like this, or don't ever learn to read like this, then they miss most of what's going on. They actually can't read very well.

If we look at a range of the best children's books published today, for example Ruth Brown's *Our Cat Flossie*, or Pamela Allen's *Fancy That!* or John Burningham's *Mr. Gumpy's Outing* and hundreds, even thousands, like them, we will see that they are books and texts of a certain kind. They have certain qualities of meaning, and particular narrative structures, where the words mean more than they say (Meek 1988). In these books picture and text counterpoint, not simply match, one another. (I have often been told that when choosing books for young readers we should make sure that the pictures match the text. This seems to me to be a very simplistic idea. In most good picture books the pictures never match the text. They tell another story. It is the trade off between them that constitutes the reading. The National Curriculum's notion of "picture cues" is similarly simplistic, as is its grasp of the reading process in general.)

Indeed the texts of these books themselves, whether there are pictures or not, are often many-layered or multivalent, and we can find many examples of innuendo, irony, metaphor, allegory. The texts are "polysemic", that is, they have hints, secrets, resonances. They make you search and reconstruct; they make you want or need to re-read, to look again, to delve, to discover and re-discover. Children have to experience these things, and learn how to handle them, because these are the basic skills of accomplished reading and, in many ways, the real teachers are the books.

As I have implied, texts can work like this in even the simplest or seemingly simplest of books, which are of course not simple at all. For young children all this happens at its best in picture books. The picture book is a particularly potent teacher of reading and everything that reading involves, because the modern picture book is a new or re-discovered art form that cues powerfully on all systems and readily makes its polysemic nature known. Such books are equally valuable for older readers, of course.

If none of this happens to children then reading does not happen, except in a very superficial way. But if we want it to happen, we have to plant the seeds of this kind of reading early, otherwise it may never grow. And we have to nourish it along the way, for example in the middle years of schooling. In other words, if we want children to read, in due course, T.S.Eliot, or James Joyce, or Bertrand Russell, or Shakespeare, with relish and understanding, or to cope expertly with their GCSE or 'A' level texts, then we must bring them up on *Our Cat Flossie, Fancy That!, Mr.*

Grumpy's Outing and the hundreds and hundreds of other books like them.

How do Reading Schemes compare?

We cannot afford to bring children up on books of lesser quality. If we look at most of the books or "readers" in most reading schemes, it becomes clear that, in the light of the two bodies of research that I have described, they do not provide the basics that children who are learning to read require. I am referring here mainly to the first few "levels" or "stages" of reading schemes like *Through the Rainbow*, *New Way*, *Reading 360*, *One, Two, Three and Away!*, *The Oxford Reading Tree*, *Language Patterns*, *Open Door* and *Reading World*.

I have, with teacher colleagues over a period of time, examined the texts of these schemes fairly closely. These are a few of our observations:

(1) Most of the books and texts in the schemes are rather nebulous and unexciting, and often relatively meaningless. The language is usually pedestrian and unadventurous. Some of the books deliberately omit punctuation, which seems astonishing (e.g. *New Way*). The illustrations are often poor, sometimes childish or garish, and there is little subtlety of trade off between print and pictures. In short, few if any of the individual books in schemes seem likely to impress themselves on children as books in their own right. As a recent investigation reported "Almost no child showed any awareness of book titles or authors" (Cato *et al*, 1992).

(2) Scheme books tend to lack variety. Some schemes claim this as a virtue, explaining that it gives children "security". So quite commonly all the books look the same and feel the same, and are the same size, and use the same kind of layout and print. (This is quite often a simplified and rather babyish style of print, lacking character and aesthetic appeal.) Often the stories have the same limited groups of characters through many books (e.g. *One, Two, Three and Away!*) frequently in the same setting. Very often book after book employs the same basic sentence pattern (e.g. *The Oxford Reading Tree*).

(3) The schemes manifestly lack books with polysemic texts, with layers of meaning, implications and secrets. They thus provide no foundation at all for more sophisticated and accomplished reading.

(4) The schemes do not envisage or encourage repeated re-readings of favourite books, which is a vital factor in learning to read (Minns, 1990). In fact the books will barely tolerate re-reading, because there is so little to discover in them. The implication is that having finished one book, you move on the next one. You would not be expected to return to an earlier book to savour it, or reconsider it. It is

difficult to imagine many of the books in reading schemes becoming established favourites or established classics, which are very important in a reading programme.

5. Overall, reading schemes appear to be designed on principles ultimately derived from behaviourist psychology. One formula that is frequently followed is "Use as few words as possible, but repeat them as often as possible". Many of the texts are in fact extremely repetitive, frequently at the expense of meaning. In some schemes virtually the same words are used and re-used in book after book (e.g. *Reading 360*). The texts are deliberately reduced to cut out the possibility of multivalent meanings. For all these reasons, the texts do not cue properly on all systems, viz.
(a) There is weak syntactic cueing, because the language is not like normal uses of written or spoken language.
(b) There is weak semantic cueing, because meaning is frequently slender, limited or even confusing.
(c) There is weak bibliographic cueing, because picture-text relationship, layout, print arrangement etc. can be misleading.
(d) On the other hand there is extreme graphophonic over-cueing with repeated words, letter groups, short patterned lines, etc.

The texts are thus hard to read normally, in a multi-cued way. In fact, the reader is forced to read by depending mainly on one cue-system (the graphophonic), which is not, as we have seen, how reading actually happens. As Henrietta Dombey has said "The complex orchestration of different kinds of information, the essential skill of reading, is not fully fostered or stimulated" (Dombey 1992).

It can be seen therefore that reading schemes are based on theoretically unsound models of reading, in spite of their repeated claims to be "scientific", "systematic" and the like. Research shows us, in fact, that using such texts with children will be bound to damage their understanding of reading and what it can be like. Many teachers compromise by using a "mixture" of reading schemes and what are called "real books" (Cato *et al*, 1992, p.23). This may well be even more damaging because, apart from the danger of presenting children with two contradictory models of the reading process (whole versus partial), it means that the books that could really teach the children are marginalised and diminished in their eyes, perhaps for ever.

It seems to me then that the texts in reading schemes are artificial texts created to fit certain psychological theories about conditioning and repetition, and about reading as a superficial decoding activity (either via whole words or blended letter sounds). These theories and the contrived texts constructed to reflect them are, I believe, mistaken when applied wholesale to reading because they exaggerate one part of the reading process to the detriment of other parts. The normal texts of childhood, or for that matter adulthood, cannot be read like this. If we neglect *Our Cat Flossie* we neglect what reading actually involves, and what we really need to teach.

References

ADAMS, M.J. (1990) *Beginning to Read: Thinking and Learning about Print* Cambridge (Mass): the MIT Press

BARRS, M. & THOMAS, A. (Eds) (1991) *The Reading Book*. London: Centre for Language in Primary Education

BROOKS, G., GORMAN, T., KENDALL, L., & TATE, A. (1992) *What Teachers in Training are Taught about Reading*. Slough, Berks: The National Foundation for Educational Research.

CATO, V., FERNANDES, C., GORMAN, T., KISPAL, A. (1992) *The Teaching of Initial Literacy: How do Teachers do it?* Slough, Berks: The National Foundation for Educational Research.

CLAY, M.M. (1991) *Becoming Literate: The Construction of Inner Control*. Birkenhead, Auckland: Heinemann

DOMBEY, H. (1992) *Words and Worlds: Reading in the Early Years of School*. Sheffield: National Association for the Teaching of English.

MARTIN, T. (1989) *The Strugglers: Working with Children who Fail to Learn to Read*. Milton Keynes: Open University Press

MEEK, M. (1988) *How Texts Teach What Readers Learn*. Stroud, Glos: The Thimble Press

MINNS, H. (1990) "In Praise of Re-reading" in *Language Matters* 1990/91 No.3

STYLES, M., BEARNE, E., & WATSON, V. (Eds) (1992) *After Alice: Exploring Children's Literature*. London: Cassell

WEAVER, C. (1988) *Reading Process and Practice: From Socio-Psycholinguistics to Whole Language*. Portsmouth, NH: Heinemann

Reading Without Words: Text and Context in the Wordless Picture Book

David Lewis

Despite the fact that the wordless book has been around in bookshops, libraries and homes for some while now I suspect that for some people the notion that one might have reading without words is not that far removed from the idea that one might have astronomy without stars or physics without matter. Others, of course, take the wordless picture book in their stride and find it wholly unremarkable - simply more evidence of the ingenuity of our talented makers of picture books. My own view is that perhaps we ought not to be surprised that such a form has emerged at the end of the twentieth century but we should certainly not take it for granted. In particular, I think there is much to be learned about stories and books in general - and about reading - from the study of such works.

Not a great deal has been written about the wordless book as a form, but this is perhaps not surprising since it is, in fact, a relatively recent development. Most, if not all, of the wordless picture books published in this country are no more than 25 years old. The first work of this kind to be published in Britain was a book entitled 'Vicky' by Renate Meyer, the widow of Charles Keeping, which appeared in 1968. Most of the titles which are now familiar to us were, in fact, produced in the seventies and and early eighties. Books such as, 'Changes, Changes' by Pat Hutchins; 'Up and Up' by Shirley Hughes; 'The Snowman' by Raymond Briggs; 'Intercity' and 'River' by Charles Keeping; 'Sunshine' by Jan Ormerod; 'Anno's Journey' and 'Anno's Britain'; and 'The Great Flood' by Peter Spier were all published in the decade from 1971 to 1981 and there is little evidence that the wholly wordless picture book was at all popular - at least in Britain - before the '70's. There is a fascinating history waiting to be written of this unusual, and wholly contemporary, form.

However, I'm not particularly concerned with history here. I want to try, in this paper, to address three related questions: first, what kind of artefact is a wordless picture book? Second, what does it mean to read one? Third, what kinds of things might we find when we observe children reading them?

The Wordless Book

What then, are the characteristics of the form? What do we mean by a book that is wordless? I think it is important to see the wordless picture book as a development that has come from within the picture story book. Picture book makers such as

Shirley Hughes and Raymond Briggs are not only superb illustrators but they are are also highly sophisticated storytellers. The wordless picture book, in their hands, is essentially an artist's solution to the task of telling a story. Their books are, therefore, not just books of pictures but sequences of images sewn together with a narrative intelligence and sensibility. Wordless picture books are what I have come to call a quasi-literary form.

Our unwritten history will one day show us how it has come about, how it is that strings of still pictures can now be articulated to create action, movement, cause, effect, feeling, intention, purpose, crisis and resolution in the mind of the sympathetic reader. The roots of the form go deep into the narrative art of the eighteenth and nineteenth centuries, into the development of caricature, the rise of the comic strip and the cartoon and, of course, more recently - and crucially - the rise and ascendency of the cinema and television.

I want to say that although in the wordless picture book we lose what we, as competent and skilled readers, are most familiar with - i.e. the words - we nonetheless retain something vital to our concept of reading, and that is the idea of structured and articulated text. The discipline of semiotics lends authority to this view for in semiotics we find a wider and more accommodating account of reading than we are, perhaps, used to operating with. Robert Hodge and Gunther Kress, in their book, *Social Semiotics*, for example, consider text to be: "... a structure of messages or message traces which has a socially ascribed unity."

They also point out that the word 'text' comes from the Latin *textus* which means 'something woven together'. The wordless picture book, I believe, sits comfortably within this definition.

Reading the Wordless Book

What does it mean, then, to read such a fabric of images? How are wordless picture books constructed so that a reader is lead to make narrative sense of sequences of still pictures? I would like to examine a short passage from Jan Ormerod's 'Sunshine' to try and illustrate how one picture book maker goes about tackling a particular narrative moment. Most readers are, I am sure, familiar with 'Sunshine', the domestic tale of the little girl and her family who wake up, have breakfast, get dressed and set off for work and for school. It is a story devoid of high drama which relies for its effect upon a close and sensitive observation of family life. As a pictorial text it is interesting because of the way in which it deploys a range of picture sequence conventions in innovative ways. To begin with, it alternates sequences of small pictures with large, full-page spreads. The sequences tend to focus upon complex physical activities such as getting dressed and they look almost as if they were a selection of still frames taken from a film. The spreads, in contrast, suggest stillness and quiet or depict moments just before some gentle activity is about to take place such as the little girl poised to climb on her parents' bed and then kissing her father to wake him up. In between these two extremes are short sequences delineating simple moments of activity such as carrying a breakfast bowl to the bedroom or climbing off the bed.

There is, however, one moment that is particularly revealing and that is the page opening where the parents realise with a start that they are late. The verso conveys agitation and panic through the startled gestures and expressions of the parents and through the contrast between the shocked parents in bed and the same scene with the bed and room empty. This dramatic contrast follows directly upon a sequence of pictures on the previous two pages showing the little girl going through the stages of getting dressed, packing her bag, reaching for a clock and calling to her parents. The last image of this sequence shows the little girl fully dressed facing out towards the reader, clock in hands, its face fully visible. She seems to be looking out beyond, or to the side of, the reader, holding the clock up for inspection. In fact, of course, she is showing the clock to her parents and over the page we see the immediate results of that last frame. This time we, as reader/viewers, are positioned behind the girl (still standing holding the clock) and in a position to register the effect that the sight of the clock has upon the parents.

The facing page depicts a scene of energetic confusion. The framing is relatively complex. The little girl stands still in the foreground and at the centre confronting the viewer and inviting the viewer's gaze, a small smile on her lips. This direct line of gaze is significant for it seems to imply an acknowledgement on the part of the depicted figure that she is being watched. She knows we are out there! The reader no longer has the sense of 'eavesdropping' on events in the book. We are invited to watch. What we see is the figure of the little girl painted in relatively saturated colour - blues, reds and greys - and this causes her to stand out from the scene, or rather, scenes behind her. Against two vacant, white frames her parents hurry to get dressed. The colours are largely pale save for the patches of the deep red towel around the father's trunk and his one red sock. Although there is only one child depicted on this page there are four parents, for two stages of getting dressed are shown. To the left of the girl, father moves to the left draped in a towel while mother moves to the right in her nightdress. To the right, time has moved on for now father moves to the right, partially dressed in shirt and sock while mother moves to the left, wrapped in a towel, turbaned and clutching a hairdryer. In both the left and right scenes the figures break the frame that strives to enclose them and this in itself suggests energy and motion. In both scenes their legs cross and this has the effect of tying them together as they apparently strain to move off in different directions. The conflicting directions are, in themselves, a source of confusion for a very persuasive signifier in picture books is that which follows the convention of left to right reading - at least in the west. Figures in motion are, more often than not, moving across the page or frame towards the right. Figures facing left are often impeded, stationary or marked out as being different in some special way. A good example of this is the moment in 'Up and Up' when the 'scientist' strides away inside an inset circle, leaving the crowds behind, to go and launch his balloon.

On this one page Jan Ormerod marshals a number of pictorial signifiers to create a scene of energetic confusion and tension - the contrary directions of movement, the broken frames, the figures held back by their overlapping limbs, the double reading of the picture plane (one child, four parents) - and yet the effect is almost sabotaged by her careful drawing. Each figure is enclosed by a clear, unbroken black line and this has the effect of freezing each individual into a statue-like pose. Ormerod's drawing has none of the energy and movement created by a looser, more flowing line (compare Quentin Blake, for example), and so, if we wish to see the full significance of the page in terms of the developing story we must override one particular convention (that which says: "unbroken lines tend to 'freeze' action") and read the rest in the light of what has gone before.

What we find when we look closely at pictures and picture sequences such as these is a weaving together of pictorial and narrative conventions to create a text of considerable richness and depth. Take, for example, point of view. It matters greatly, both in pictures and in prose, from what angle, perspective and direction a scene has been constructed. Ormerod is extremely skilful at manipulating the reader/viewer's point of view in the few pages we have just been considering. We move from an external viewpoint as we observe the little girl getting dressed to the viewpoint of the parents when we see the clock face held up for inspection (quite a subtle move this one for we are only likely to see this shift in viewpoint on a second or third reading). Over the page we shift again to a rear view of the girl - we can now see what she can see, her parents' shock and surprise and then, finally, we are once again external to the family group, though this time drawn by the little girl's gaze into a relationship of complicity - thus we are led to see the parents not just from the outside but as the little girl 'sees' them.

But that's not all, of course. Much more is going on besides. Colour, light, shade, framing, the relative sizes of objects within the frame, gesture, posture and facial expression - all of these things are features of the textual fabric and all contribute to the narrative sense that the reader is invited to build. The American writer and critic Perry Nodelman, in his book 'Words about Images', offers an extensive analysis of the codes of pictorial signification to be found in picture books, but the most engaging and persuasive account by a British writer of what is involved in reading pictures in picture books is probably that of Judith Graham in her work *Pictures on the Page'.*

Children Reading a Wordless Book

I now want to turn to the question of what we might learn when we invite children to read wordless picture books with us. I want to share with you some thoughts that arose from the analysis of conversations with three children who were asked to read a wordless picture book with me. The book, 'Where is Monkey?' by Dieter Schubert, is not particularly well known and, in fact, was unknown to the three children at the time of reading. The readings took place some years ago when the children were six and were part of a study involving a group of infant children reading and listening to a range of picture books. The three children involved are Malcolm, Nathaniel and Jane.

But first a cautionary note. We must, I think, draw a clear distinction between the notion of reading a wordless picture book to oneself on the one hand, and reading such a book 'aloud' on the other. As long as reading involves no more than the process of an individual's making sense of textual matter then there seems to be no great problem involved, but when we mean the production of an oral text on the basis of a pictorial one then the processes involved seem to be more like a kind of free translation than a straightforward 'reading', In asking Jane, Malcolm and Nathaniel to 'tell the story' of 'Where is Monkey?' I could only be inviting them to tell a story on the basis of their understanding and interpretation of the picture sequences. Their oral tales stand in a very different relation to the primary text than would be the case with the more familiar oral reading of a verbal text. Each child tells a slightly different story and there can be no question of any one of the stories being more correct or accurate than any other.

Nonetheless, from the children's tellings we might learn something of how as readers and tellers, they go about the process of constructing a story; what kinds of knowledge they bring to bear on and through their interpretations and to which of the many pictorial codes they appear to be sensitive. Reflected in the children's tellings we might also expect to learn something of the nature of the pictorial text before them and thus more of the nature of picture book text in general. What we may not suppose is that what they say is what they see, as their perceptions and their readings may not always be registered within their tellings. At any point they may choose to be silent.

Let me briefly describe 'Where is Monkey?' so that we have a sense of how the pictorial text proceeds. In outline, the story revealed by the picture sequences appears to be about a little boy who, on a trip to a park or wood to feed the geese with his mother, or an older female friend or relative, drops and loses his cuddly toy monkey. Despite a search in the rain they fail to find monkey even though he is lying not far from where they are looking at the base of a hollow tree. Some mice find the toy, drag it into the tree and proceed to play roughly with it. In doing so they break off its tail. Once they have tied its tail together again they use it to block up the entrance when a hedgehog tries to force its way in. The hedgehog claims the monkey and takes it back to its family where, once again, it is treated very roughly. A magpie next claims it after scaring away the hedgehogs and takes it back to its nest where it proceeds to pull out one of the shiny eyes. Monkey is then dropped into the pond below from where he is rescued accidentally by an old gentleman who is fishing. The old man appears to be a toy maker, or mender, for he takes monkey back to a small dolls' hospital where he washes and repairs him then sits him in the window of his shop facing the street. The little boy eventually reclaims his monkey once he has recognised it through the shop window. The book ends with an image of monkey and child reunited.

I asked Malcolm, Nathaniel and Jane - along with some of their classmates - to 'tell me the story' and their different versions, along with the conversations woven around them, were very revealing. In particular I was struck by the different ways in which they went about telling their stories and I want to finish this paper by describing and analysing these three quite distinct styles. I have borrowed this terminology from the work of Bussis et al (1985) reported in their book *'Enquiry into Meaning'* for it seems to me that there are interesting parallels between the 'styles' of learning to read exhibited by the children studied by the research team and the 'styles' of reading and telling adopted by the children with whom I worked. *'Enquiry into Meaning'* is not now readily available but the work is extensively cited and discussed in Barrs and Thomas (Eds) (1991).

Of the three children, Malcolm and Nathaniel were the most conversational in the sense that they were keen to involve me in the telling of the story. Characteristically, Malcolm would do this through sprinkling tag questions amongst his observations and statements ("They're not that far away from him are they?", "Looks like he's going to tread on it doesn't he?") whereas Nathaniel slipped in and out of his story through text-to-life references and life-to-text anecdotes ("When soft toys get wet they're easy to come apart when they're only made of wool"). In contrast to these dialogic modes Jane's telling was as monologic as it could possibly be, my role being reduced to the very occasional interjection. From the beginning it was clear that she saw the task as 'telling a story', complete and whole and she put a good deal of energy into producing a seamless narrative text ("Well, first of all the little boy puts the monkey...").

Jane achieved this cohesion largely through a reliance upon the connectives "and", "and then", "then after that" and so on but she did attain a certain narrative density through such cohesive ties as "and so", "because", "who". Malcolm too attended closely to narrative meanings but his telling was the sparest of the three. His narration came in short bursts, brief statements about pictures or groups of pictures that often omitted the subject ("...getting monkey out of bed", "...jumping on him", "...stitching it up"). His sense of the dynamics of the story emerged largely through his bold use of intonation and stress. Both Malcolm and Jane were extremely adept at summarising ensembles and sequences of pictures, Jane being particularly good at rapidly getting to the heart of an image, sometimes pulling together the accumulating meanings of the story in a single word or phrase. Most notably she was able to do this at the moment when the monkey is taken home by the old gentleman. In her apparently throwaway phrase "...luckily it's a toy mender" she correctly interpreted the essentially arcane symbolism of the dolls' hospital sign, gathered up all the accumulated vicissitudes of the mauled and battered toy and pointed towards a happy resolution. Her "luckily" is pregnant with narrative significance.

Jane and Malcolm differed, however, in their response to ambiguity in the pictures. Malcolm wore his doubt on his sleeve, so to speak, openly admitting he was unsure what was going on, or asking questions - half to himself and half to me - in search of clarification ("What're they doing here? Taking off his clothes. What're they doing now?"). Jane, in contrast, was so dedicated to a continuous narration that there was no opportunity to express doubt or hesitation. She would self-correct what she perceived to be her misreadings of certain pictures not by going back and starting again but by incorporating another small step in the narrative, thus maintaining the flow and 'explaining' the anomaly produced by her 'error'.

Nathaniel was far less aware of the inconsistencies produced by his occasional misreadings than either Jane or Malcolm and this blind spot seemed to be largely the result of a close focus upon local detail within each picture. He seemed far less aware of the developing shape of his story than the others and his curiosity about, and fascination with, individual picture elements and his tendency to lapse into anecdote led him into some amusing interpretations and the occasional gross blunder. Twice, for example, he failed to follow the basic book-reading rule - which applies to wordless books as much as to the more conventional kind - that the eye's left to right progress across the verso page ends at, or before, the gutter and returns to the left margin at the next row below. One might be tempted to say that this kind of error reveals Nathaniel to be an inexperienced and thus inept reader but there is much evidence in the transcripts of his reading - both of this book and of others - that he is possessed of a high degree of interpretive sensitivity. For example, the open textured quality of his reading, the way he moved in and out of the story with ease, combined with his immense curiosity about detail, lead him to offer a denser, richer reading of events. He was aware of what we might call 'sub-plots' in the picture sequences whereas Malcolm and Jane were rather blinkered by comparison. He is also extremely knowledgeable about stories and books and time and again offered glimpses of his intertextual understanding. In the present case he immediately saw the similarity between the toy mender and Geppetto from 'Pinocchio'.

In these similarities and differences we get some sense of the range of things that the young reader of a wordless book does to make narrative sense of sequences of pictures. There is the need for attention to the trajectory of the story, the patterns and twists and turns that the narrative takes - What Barrs and Thomas refer to as the 'big shapes', - but there is also the need for attention to small things, for not only does the unfolding of the tale ultimately depend upon the articulation of detail but also the depth and range of its meanings, its metaphorical reach and its narrative texture. And these are lessons that apply as much to books with words as to those without.

References

BARRS, M. & THOMAS, A. (Eds) (1991) *The Reading Book*, Centre for Language in Primary Education

BUSSIS, A., CHITTENDEN, E., AMAREL, M. & KLAUSNER, E. (1985) *Enquiry into Meaning: an Investigation of Learning to Read*, Lawrence Erlbaum Associates

GRAHAM, J. (1990) *Pictures on the Page*, NATE

HODGE, R. & KRESS, G. (1988) *Social Semiotics*, Polity Press

NODELMAN, P. (1988) *Words about Pictures: the Narrative Art of Children's Picture Books*, University of Georgia Press

Texts that Persuade

Bob Leather & Tony Martin

In 'Readers and Texts' (Martin & Leather, 1992) we described work carried out with both adults and primary school children in which we investigated how they 'read' the openings of novels. As a result we developed a model of the reading process which took account of both sides of this process - the reader and the text. The different facets of the model can be found in the earlier article, but basically it can be represented as:

READER ------- INTERACTION ------- TEXT

The interaction is the result both of what the text brings to the reader and what the reader takes into the text. Texts only comes alive in the minds of readers and different readers bring different lives, opinions, beliefs and personalities to texts. Hence the different readings by different readers of the same text. While being fascinated by the part played by readers in the reading process and arguing for this to be given more attention and status in schools we also became increasingly aware of the demands of the text. A close examination of the openings we used illustrated the ways in which they worked and the conventions which readers have to appreciate if they are to make their way through them successfully. This in turn led us to consider the demands made on readers by different texts and whether we therefore read different types of text in different ways.

Our focus shifted, then, to an examination of how readers respond to two different types of text - poetry and advertising. We are well aware that there is no way we can really find out how a reader responds to the text. We cannot get inside a reader's head as s/he is reading. Nevertheless we can investigate what readers are conscious of trying to do as they read as well as examining the texts to see what demands they make on those who read them. This may well have important implications for how we approach aspects of reading in the classroom.

Poetry

We worked with both adults and primary school children, providing them with photocopies of poems printed on A4 sheets. We asked them to jot down, around the poems, whatever was going on in their minds as they were reading. When we had worked previously with the opening of novels we had been aware of the difficulty of convincing our readers that we did not have a particular agenda in mind. Comments such as, "Well, I've done it, but I'm not sure if it is what you want." indicated a concern that there were right and wrong ways of responding. The children had initially viewed the whole business as a comprehension exercise in disguise! We felt that with poetry this was liable to be a major issue, perhaps with the adults' memories of Eng.Lit. forcing them down a particular path so that they ignored what they were actually thinking and feeling. How we read is influenced by our knowledge that what we are reading is a poem, but this in turn will be due to how we have been taught. All we could do was emphasise, 'Whatever enters your head, jot it down!'

The adults formed two distinct groups. Firstly there were some who freely admitted not reading much poetry. In fact some had not read a poem for some years - since leaving school. Secondly there was a group from Cove Cottage in Grasmere, Cumbria, the former home of the poet Wordsworth. These were all English graduates for whom poetry was a major part of their lives. We wondered if there would be any similarities or differences in the way they read poetry. They all had the same four poems, chosen to represent differences in both subject matter and style. Analysing their readings was fascinating as at first there appeared to be little common ground amongst any of them! Indeed, though we did eventually tease out some general issues, the main impression is of different individuals responding in different, personal ways to the poems. So much seemed to be going on as these readers made their way through the poems that we were forced to question some of the practices which go on in schools with regard to the teaching of poetry.

Out of these different readings we found particular readers leaning towards distinct ways of responding and identified seven 'categories' of reader. Some readers fell exactly into one of these categories, while others showed a tendency to do so but also included elements of the other categories in their readings.

THE FREEWHEELER ... read at the level of word association, so that a word or phrase would set off a personal association which had nothing to do with the subject matter of the poem! The phrase 'six white geese' produced the response 'six geese a-laying, five gold rings' and the word 'force' in Ted Hughes' 'Wind' produced 'Darth Vader - may the force be with you'. There is no doubt that we all respond like this, almost subconsciously, as we read, but whether it should be encouraged in the classroom is an interesting thought.

THE LIFER ... made connections between the poem and the reader's life. One of the readers had been on holiday in Scotland and had visited Inversnaid. Hopkins' poem 'Inversnaid' produced an excited response as the verses triggered memories of the holiday, 'Our first sighting of wild goats as we approached Inversnaid'. Charles Causley's 'Dora' produced the response 'First World War - my father's shrapnel wound'. A slightly different life response was apparent through such comments as 'Rather sad - I should hate to feel like that', the reader putting herself in the situation the poem is describing. Again we all do this, indeed it is one of the most powerful aspects of response.

Both of these types of reading draw attention to the part played by the reader - the left hand side of the model. We would argue that there is still a need for this aspect of reading to be given more status in teaching. There is a danger that we only focus on the text without investigating what brings it to life in the mind of the reader. However on their own these responses are inadequate because they fail to account for how the text works. Indeed the freewheeler and the lifer frequently ignore the text altogether. Even the response 'Rather sad' begs the question as to how the text manages to make the reader feel sad.

The following two categories focussed completely on the text, not giving any indication of a 'personal' response at all. We would suggest them to be as inadequate as the two above.

THE TRANSLATOR ... tried to explain what the poem was about, paraphrasing the text. A verse of Ted Hughes' 'Wind' was 'translated' as 'Day break brought a change in the weather - wind still strong'. Viewing the poem as a comprehension exercise could be due to years of such work in school or perhaps just an understandable response to a text that the reader finds difficult.

TRAINED READERS ... felt that poems had to be approached in specific ways, reflecting how they had been taught. Indeed one wrote, 'This is a good poem. And I'm aware that I read as a trained reader - that my thoughts are in/on the poem - I cut out the extraneous before the object'. There were two types of trained reader.

THE TEXTER ... focused on how the poem 'worked', with comments such as, 'Language highlights the fact of the poem - I like 'flutes' - breaks the role of the verse'. In addition texters made intertextual references such as 'The tarot pack makes me think of T.S.Eliot (Madam Sosostris in The Waste Land)', referring to their previous literary experience.

THE TECHNIQUE SPOTTER ... simply picked out poetic techniques with comments such as 'vivid use of metaphor'. This seemed an arid exercise in that it did not get beyond the simple recognition of the technique. No mention of how the technique worked and the effect it had. Adjectives such as 'vivid' tell us nothing.

Finally we had one reader who responded at a personal level but then tried to examine how the poem was working in order to affect her in such ways. Equal weight was given both the part played by the reader and the demands of the text. We gave her the title 'COMPLETE READER' not because her responses were totally 'complete' (could they ever be?) but because her readings reflected both sides of the model. A comment on Gillian Clarke's 'Overheard in County Sligo' exemplifies her approach:

'A very empty desolate life ... this all seems reflected by the repetitive rhyme and rhythm of the poem. No sense of hope or change. Very simple rhyme scheme and the poem ends where it started as if it will be repeated again and again. Her life will never change.'

This reader was from Dove Cottage. Apart from her, if any generalisation can be made it was that this group tended to concentrate their attentions on the text rather than their personal responses, while the other group contained a wider variety of readings.

When we examined the responses of nine, ten and eleven year old children we found only one of the above readers represented. These were LIFERS with comments such as 'I would not do that'. In addition there were a few (but only a few) observations on the quality of the text (e.g. 'Not a very interesting line') but none of the children could be described as TEXTERS. However, there were two types of reader which did stand out.

IMAGERS .... described the pictures in the mind which were created by the poems. Comments such as: 'I can see an old woman walking in a gale with the hairy toe' indicated this process but in addition some children chose to draw pictures around the poems. Imaging is recognised as something we all do when we read and it was surprising that it was hardly mentioned by our adult readers.

QUESTIONERS .... asked questions of the text, seemingly feeling as if they were not being given enough information. In Charles Causley's 'Timothy Winters', the opening line: 'Timothy Winters comes to school', provoked questions such as" 'Who is he?' and 'What school?' A major aspect of the reading process is the way readers fill the gaps in the text and most poetry contains more gaps than narrative. We learn to accept the poem as it stands and do not expect the background information supplied in novels but we only learn this through reading a wide range of poetry. The popularity of narrative poetry with children, from traditional ballads to many of Michael Rosen's poems, is perhaps something to do with there being fewer gaps. Perhaps some of our adult readers had lots of questions but did not want to admit this. It may have accounted for the TRANSLATORS.

Advertising

Adverts and poems are, of course, very different in both form and function. Or are they? We used the title 'Texts that Persuade' for this article because it seemed to us that both types of text do, in their different ways attempt to do just that. Obviously the advertiser wants to get us to buy a particular product and does so by trying to convince us we need it to enhance our lives. But it is interesting to note that many of the techniques used in advertisements are also the stock-in-trade of the poet. It would also be true to say, we believe, that part of the function of many poems is to persuade us that a particular description can change how we perceive the world.

The techniques shared by poets and advertisers, such as rhyme, alliteration, syntactic and typographical patterning, puns, images and so on, are all meant to catch our eyes and ears and engage our sensibilities in order to bring about the changes noted above. Of course, the greater the poet and the more skilful the copywriter, the less we are likely to be aware of the surface techniques which are merely the means for achieving deeper ends.

We wanted to find out how far adults and children were aware of some of the techniques used by advertisers and whether they could articulate how and why the techniques were being used. In addition, we were curious to discover whether advertising texts were 'read' in the same ways as literary texts.

Four adverts were selected from a variety of sources: 'Radio Times', a weekend colour supplement, a woman's weekly magazine and one from the new generation of magazines aimed at the affluent male. The adults were given exactly the same instructions as for the poems.

What was fascinating about their responses was that it proved possible to categorise them in exactly the same way as for the poetry responses with the addition of one new category. A selection of comments is given below under the appropriate categories.

FREEWHEELER ... The sort of unfocused response apparent in some of the responses to poems also cropped up in the comments about adverts. Thus, the word 'licence' in one advert encouraged the contextually irrelevant response 'car' in one reader. Of more interest, were the freewheeling responses which the advertisement for Lotus cars stimulated. The Lotus logo which encloses the name of the company brought out the following comments: 'speed', 'Dream car£££££s', and the following was one reader's reaction to the complete advert which contained a colour photograph of a young man driving among lakes and mountains: 'That's me in 5 years driving round Windermere'.

LIFER ... As discussed in the previous section, a 'lifer' is someone who sees in a text a direct link with their own life experience. Several readers provided comments under this heading. One of our adverts was for the Halifax Building Society. The opening sentence in the main text read: 'When your kids leave home why not live a little'. One reader wrote: 'My parents are doing. They're never in when I phone.'

TRANSLATOR ... Few of our readers felt the need to paraphrase sections of text in adverts. We only found one example. Presumably most readers find such texts relatively straightforward with no need for translation.

TEXTER ... Again, few of our readers made comments here. The Lotus advert which contained some technical language needing a specialist knowledge produced the following: 'Trying to impress with jargon that doesn't necessarily mean anything.'

A lengthy double page advert for the Post Office in the form of a short story did not impress some of our readers. One response was: 'No punchy lines - not a good advert, very unclear.'

TECHNIQUE SPOTTER ... This category only brought forward one comment, which was about a lengthy Post Officer advert: 'a narrative'.

In summary, most of the comments were to be found under the FREEWHEELER and LIFER categories. But there were quite a number of comments that could be grouped together into a category which had no parallel in the poetry responses. In several of the adverts our readers challenged statements and claims made by the advertiser. This particularly applied to statements in an advert for Carnation Slender. The following example indicates the bluntness of some of the responses. The claim" 'Be up to 4lbs lighter a week from today', received the comment 'lies' from one reader.

Similarly, some readers felt able to pass judgements about the whole message in some adverts: 'sick', 'eyewash' and 'Aah! How sweet', were some of the comments recorded. We would characterize such comments as PERSONAL JUDGEMENT and distinguish them from the comments made by the TRAINED READER by emphasising that the personal judgements were made from the perspective of the reader whereas the trained readers' comments were more text-referenced.

We used a somewhat different approach to the advertising texts when working with a group of Year 6 pupils in a small school in Cumbria. Initially, we played them a videotape of a number of adverts chosen at random. The tape contained about ten minutes of adverts. We followed this up with a group discussion and then asked the pupils to choose one of the adverts to write about. Later, we gave the group four printed adverts for products which we thought would be of interest to them. We asked them to record their impressions about one of these.

Watching the videotape with the pupils proved an absorbing experience. Their reactions to individual adverts demonstrated how powerful and successful this type of persuasion is. The children laughed at the antics of 'characters' involved in the adverts, recited whole chunks of discourse in unison from adverts they were familiar with, and joined in the chorus from the Ford advert: 'Everything we do is driven by you'. They might have been watching well-loved films, sitcoms or soaps or listening to popular records. Indeed, they wanted us to play more recordings after Break and were disappointed that we hadn't got any more to offer them!

Several of the oral and written responses from pupils could be classed within or LIFER category, as indicated by the following:

I know they're good trainers because lots of people buy them and they're trendy too.

Of particular interest during the discussion were the comments about an advertisement for Pepsi which featured Michael Jackson. The children were full of stories about the supposed disfigurement to Michael Jackson's face as a result of plastic surgery. Such stories seemed to add to his mystique. Like the FREEWHEELING comments from adults, the pupils' remarks indicated the success of the advertiser in removing the reader/viewer from the here-and-now to a fantasy world through the use of verbal and visual images. However, one pupil wrote later that the offer made on the Pepsi advert for free tickets to a Michael Jackson concert was not all it might seem:

I liked the Michael Jackson advert because it had Michael Jackson in it. But the advert when it was about Pepsi was a bit of a bribe. It was a bribe because if you like Michael Jackson you would want to go and see him in a concert. And by going to see him you would have to buy a Pepsi can because you could win something to see him.

We think we follow the argument! From the discussion it was clear that the young lady who wrote the above knew that advertisers do not offer something for nothing.

Most of the pupils in the group had similar confidence in refuting the claims of advertisers in much the same way as our adult readers in the PERSONAL JUDGEMENT category. A further example illustrates personal judgement being supported by life experience:

The M and M advert is good because I love M and Ms. the bit what says the milk chocolate melts in your hand isn't true. I put lots of M and Ms in my hand and held them for a while and whatever colour the M and M was that colour was all over my hand.

Conclusions

It was very noticeable that there were far fewer comments about advertising texts than about novels or poems, both from our adult and pupil readers. This may have been due to the fact that advertising texts are so much more part of our everyday lives than literary texts that we can 'read' them much more easily and less carefully, perhaps. On the other hand, it may have been due to the fact that neither adults nor children have a framework for discussing media texts whereas there is an established routine for discussing poetry and novels.

If the latter is the case, we feel strongly that teachers should begin to use media texts of all kinds in primary classrooms in order to discuss some of the ways in which such texts are constructed. Useful questions to ask would be: What is the text about? Who has written/spoken the text and what sort of relationship is there between the author and the reader/listener? What is the function of the language in the text?

A further feature of the responses we obtained to our texts was the confidence of readers to pass judgements about the advertisements compared with the reluctance to express personal views about literary texts. We believe that teachers must encourage the development of a more personal response to literature in the classroom with less emphasis on literary techniques, something which seems to us to weaken poetry in particular as an experience. The spontaneous responses to hearing catching songs, puns and slogans on video reminded us how much enjoyment there can be for children in the sheer sound of language.

Conversely, we believe that teaching children something about the language of advertising is important. If we teach something about the techniques behind the message we are empowering them to make rational rather than emotional judgements. In effect, we are developing strategies for enabling them to RESIST such texts, whereas in our approach to poetry we are trying to encourage INVOLVEMENT.

Reference

MARTIN, T. & LEATHER, B. (1992) 'Readers and texts', in Satow, F. & Gatherer, W. (eds) *Literacy without Frontiers* Widnes: UKRA

The Genre Debate in the UK

Alison Littlefair

The debate about genre began in Australia in the 1980s where it has resulted in considerable tensions. There is an academic linguistic debate and an educational debate which concerns how we use this knowledge in our teaching of writing.

The academic debate concerns the way we choose the language we use. Genre theorists state that our purpose dictates how we organise our speaking and learning and that our experience has taught us either explicitly or implicitly these ways of communication. They go on to describe the characteristic linguistic features of these language forms or genres.

The education debate in Australia is about the teaching of writing and, indeed, the role of the teacher. It has been mainly between those who hold that a process writing approach is paramount and those who wish to introduce a more structured approach. There has been considerable anxiety that a child-centred approach of encouraging children's personal development and written creativity be maintained. Genre theorists are certainly not denying the importance of children's written creativity but they state that children should be taught a range of genres. They also insist on the right of children to be taught more formal ways of communication in our society, adding that once children have this knowledge they can utilise it for their own purposes.

I want to look at the educational debate, which has already begun in this country, about whether genre is a useful, valuable concept for the classroom. We could say that we already have considerable awareness of the importance of children writing and reading for a range of purposes and within different contexts. On the other hand, perhaps we need more knowledge about the kinds of texts which our children write.

The background in Australia and in the UK

It seems to me that the genre debate in this country is taking place against a somewhat different background from the one in Australia.

Australia

During the 1980s Donald Graves (1983) greatly influenced the teaching of writing in Australian primary schools. There was emphasis on a whole language approach. Teachers became interested in the writing process rather than simply considering the product of children's writing. Teachers held conferences with individual children and encouraged them to discuss WHAT they were writing about.

At the same time Halliday was continuing his research into the implication of linguistic thought for language learning and teaching both as Professor of Linguistics at Sydney University and as consultant to the Curriculum Development Centre's Language Development Project. Halliday organised Language in Education Conferences to bring together teachers, and linguists to discuss matters of mutual concern. They were mainly interested in the ideas of the systemic school of linguistics which look at the interactive patterns of the language we use for different purposes in varying situations.

In Sydney, linguists and teachers began an investigation in classrooms of the variety of children's writing. An enormous number of scripts written by children was studied and categorised into different genres according to the writing purpose. The linguists and teachers then studied the scripts in order to describe how each genre of writing was organised. In other words, how children had organised their meanings in written language. Thus attention was directed to the text, that is the product of children's writing.

Genrists became convinced that many young children only experience writing a narrow range of genres. In fact, they suggested that many young children only wrote stories. They concluded that teachers should become more interventionist and teach children the form of less familiar genres such as simple explanatory reports and descriptions. Thus the perspective of whole language enthusiasts and those exploring genre ideas were at opposite ends of a continuum of teaching priorities and a 'head on' clash was perhaps inevitable.

United Kingdom

Donald Graves (1983) was also influential in developing attitudes in this country to the teaching of writing but perhaps not to the same extent as in Australia. Genre ideas are emerging here against a background of research into the teaching of writing and into language education.

We can trace a range of influences in the teaching of writing in the UK: the work of James Moffett (1968) in the USA, the Schools Council Project on Writing across the Curriculum (Britton et al, 1975), the Crediton Project (Wilkinson et al, 1980). The more recent work of the National Writing Project has emphasised the importance of writing purposes, of context and of writing for different audiences.

There have also been government reports about the teaching of language itself. The

Bullock Report (DES, 1975) emphasised the importance of language in education. The Kingman Report (DES, 1988) looked at the model of language most appropriate for education. The Cox Reports (DES, 1988 & 1989) recommended how teaching the four language modes of reading, writing, speaking and listening should be approached emphasising the importance of context, audience and purpose. The National Curriculum for English (DES, 1989) made most of these recommendations statutory.

However, there is little in the statutory orders which really explains why concepts like 'context, audience and purpose' are important in language education. It was the brief of the Language in the National Curriculum Project to provide relevant in-service for teachers. Many teachers have already benefitted from LINC's in-service work (Carter, 1990) which has included many ideas from genre theory.

Already, concern has been voiced. Some (Dixon & Stratta, 1993) suggest that genre ideas oppose much of the 1970s research (Britton et al, 1975) into writing development. Others (Barrs, 1992) fear a return to prescriptive language teaching with concentration on the product rather than the process.

Before we engage in this debate we should look quickly at the concepts themselves.

A brief look at genre and register

When we refer to 'genre ideas' we are usually also referring to the concept of 'register'. 'Genre' itself is a misleading term for we already have an understanding of genre as a text type or category. The linguistic view, however, is far more abstract than this. It refers to a social process. In other words, when we communicate we follow some kind of pattern which we have learned as members of a culture. So when I planned this paper my experience of writing similar papers and listening to papers provided me with implicit knowledge of how to go about planning the framework:

> background in Australia and the UK
> basic concepts
> looking at the arguments
> suggesting further implications for a way forward

This is a framework of the meanings which I want to express. Clearly this is not a rigid structure for it is my individual plan but it is influenced by my prior knowledge of how to go about the task. I would describe this genre as 'conference paper'. I am not slavishly following a structure because the meanings I want to impart are individual.

I also had to fill in the details of the framework. These details concern my subject, the linguistic mode I choose and my audience. They are the features of the context within which I am working. In responding to these features I will choose a language variety, or register, and express it through my choice of vocabulary and grammar. If I were chatting to a friend at a party my choice of vocabulary and grammar would be different.

Halliday (Halliday & Hasan, 1989) suggests that any communicative situation can be analysed in terms of what it is about (field of discourse), the method or mode of communication (mode of discourse) and who the communication is for (tenor of discourse). These three factors together produce a register which we express through a choice of vocabulary and grammar. So there is not an ad hoc choice of language but neither is there any rigid direction of linguistic choice.

This linguistic description indicates the importance of social purpose, of context and of audience and explains why we choose the language we do in different situations.

The Debate: lack of consensus of opinion

There is comment (Dixon and Stratta, 1993) that there is no consensus of opinion about genres. This is true because the academic debate is dynamic. Gunther Kress notes: 'The debate ranges from a position which treats genres as fully determined in all essential characteristics and therefore as outside the scope of effective individual action, to positions which treat genres as relatively fluid structures, subject to the actions of socially located individual agents. In this view the fluidity of genre derives from a complex of social factors.' (Kress, 1989:11).

So there are varying pockets of agreement. On the whole we are probably happy to leave the linguistic argument to the linguists and concentrate on what the general notion has to offer our work within the classroom.

The question of purpose

Most genrists, although not Hasan, see purpose as determining the genre. Here is a bone of contention. Dixon and Stratta (1993) suggest that if purpose determines genre then there must be countless genres each with their own structure - clearly this would result in an impossible teaching situation. It is more sensible to look at a manageable base of broad writing purposes and therefore at broad genre categories where we can make some predictions about their form. When necessary we can look at a particular genre if that is a helpful thing to do.

The question of distinctive patterns.

Once we begin to refer to genres as having characteristic patterns we have problems. There is the likelihood that we will note the distinctive pattern of a particular genre and teach it rigidly. But this is to misunderstand the flexibility of a genre. Every text has characteristic features which Hasan (1978) has called 'obligatory features' or we would not recognise its type. Hasan also notes 'optional features' which depend on the purpose of our communication and our personal interpretation of the meaning. Genres are not rigid; rather they are dynamic purposeful activities. They alter as the ways in which we express meaning alter.

Too much linguistic detail?

Sheeran and Barnes (1991) suggest that the disadvantage of genres is that they are tied too closely to register. They refer to the need to teach secondary school children 'the ground rules' which they describe as being concerned with meaning rather than with linguistic detail. However, most genrists would say that you cannot simply teach a structure of meaning without including the actual linguistic expression of that meaning. As we alter the meaning we wish to express we alter the genre or the register or both - it depends on our purpose.

The debate: links between spoken and written language

There is the argument that children learn to use a range of registers of language through being exposed to them. It is clear that children within a rich language environment learn a great deal about the way in which language works. Children imitate the way in which they hear language being used. Spoken language has an immediate audience and there is the dynamic of conversation. I do not think that we can assume that most children have the same immersion into the registers of written language.

Margaret Donaldson (1988) highlights the difference between spoken and written language by describing the latter as 'disembedded'. In other words written language is usually independent of any immediate context which may in itself prove to be a difficulty. We may well have to help children make links between spoken and written language by strategies like sharing reading with children both as teachers and parents.

The debate: teaching writing

Informed choice

The work of the Schools Council Development Project on Writing across the Curriculum (Britton, J. et al, 1975) encouraged us to be clear about the purposes of children's writing tasks and to be aware that different purposes result in different kinds of writing. However, we did not consider the characteristic language features of each category. Linguistic insights now suggest that we should think about the choices of genre form and of vocabulary and grammar which children make as they write. Certainly attention will be paid to the product of children's writing. However, that is not to dismiss the importance of the writing process for the real concern is how meaning is expressed.

Barrs (1992) accuses Australian genrists like Frances Christie, Joan Rothery and Jim Martin of laying down the law and of having contempt for modern approaches to teaching writing and certainly their writing is forthright. Sheeran and Barnes (1991:108) condemn genre strategies. They state: 'The writing process ceases to be creative and interactive, the genre no longer a facilitator in a state of flux and development but a rigid straight-jacket to constrain rather than liberate it.'

There is, in fact, choice involved in writing genres. The choice, however, is not open ended because once we have a purpose for writing our choice of genre form and choice of vocabulary and grammar becomes certainly restricted but not formulaic. We are used to discussing the content of writing tasks with children. We can also discuss how to express that content. Such teaching calls for professional implementation of linguistic knowledge to help young writers express their meaning.

Writing development

There was an assumption in the Schools Council 1970s work that children gradually developed the ability and understanding necessary to write formally. Expressive writing was seen as the basis of other kinds of writing. Genre ideas challenge this assumption by suggesting that context can provide the stimulus for writing and that we can encourage children to write formally from quite an early stage in writing development.

Such a suggestion challenges a more child-centred approach where emphasis is placed on the child's interest initiating writing purposes. Genrists suggest that we can provide contexts which, together with the teacher's suggestions and guidance, steer young writers into widening their repertoire. Perhaps we need to value more formal writing as much as imaginative and creative writing. Indeed, by extending young children's awareness of written forms we are providing a bedrock upon which children can use imagination and creativity.

The debate: is 'genre' just about writing?

There is criticism (Barrs 1992) that work about genre in Australia has concentrated on writing. This is, of course, fair comment but there has been research in this country into children's awareness of reading different genres and registers.

Research at the Open University, for example, suggested that less able readers of Years 5, 7 and 9 seemed to have far less awareness of language variation than average and able readers of the same ages (Littlefair 1991). Chapman (1987) found that many less able readers' ability actually decreased after their entry into the secondary school, an indication of the problems posed by the range of subject texts which they meet.

Insights into strategies of teaching reading

Some children seem able to develop an implicit awareness of language variation but it does seem that the majority of pupils would enhance their reading development if they were helped to greater understanding and awareness of the different ways in which authors use language.

The Open University research (Littlefair, 1991) also suggested that it is helpful to categorise books into major genre categories: literary, expository, procedural and reference. These categories are based on the main purpose of the writer and the way in which that purpose is expressed linguistically. Sometimes the writing purpose and the linguistic expression are not synonymous. There is no blueprint, of course, of how writers organise their work but it is important that we are aware of what reading experience we are providing for our children. For instance, we may think we are providing plenty of opportunity for children to read explanation and description when in fact the writer has chosen to explain in the register and genre of a procedural text. We can also monitor the balance of children's reading of stories and non-narrative genres of books.

Teachers' knowledge of genre and register can also inform their selection of books. In particular, this knowledge is valuable when we select simplified information books for young children to read. We may have to decide whether we wish our younger readers to read information books which are written as stories or whether we wish them to begin to cope with the language of explanation and description. We need linguistic knowledge that will help us to make these kinds of judgements.

The debate: reading and writing formal language

When children begin to read non-narrative, they encounter the language of books and for some it will be a first meeting. Most children are very familiar with the form of a story. They anticipate that one event will follow another and are caught up in the dynamics of this genre. They are not nearly so familiar with the form of an explanatory or descriptive genre where there is a logical presentation of information rather than a time sequence of events. How can these readers begin to predict the way the text is organised?

Just how far should we explicitly teach our pupils to read and write more formal genres of language? This kind of language is far removed from spoken language. It is the 'language of systematic thought' which Margaret Donaldson (1988) considers essential if children are to extend their reasoning abilities. She notes (1988:27): 'The ability to deal with sophisticated impersonal prose of the kind we have been considering does not leap up suddenly when needed like the genie from Aladdin's lamp. It is the outcome of years of sustained direction towards an ultimate goal. If primary teachers do not recognise this, they are failing to see the scope and reach of their own importance."

The debate: integrated language work

As children read and write about information they meet more formal texts. We can familiarise children with a range of genres and registers by inter-relating reading and writing activities, and by talking about different ways of expression. Cambourne & Brown (1989) refer to the notion of 'immersion' into a range of genres and registers. Knowledge about genre can inform our approach to topic work. We may reconsider the assumptions we make when we ask pupils to, 'Write it in your own words'.

Integrated language work is not restricted to the primary school for it has enormous implications in the secondary school. The Bullock Report indicated the importance of language across the curriculum in secondary schools. Different subjects have characteristic vocabulary and characteristic forms of expression. Subject teachers themselves are not always aware of these characteristics but we now have insights which can help. We have to look how linguistic form and choice of vocabulary and grammar express the concepts within specialist subjects. Clearly more research is necessary in this area.

Conclusion

Perhaps the debate about genre is really about how we impart knowledge. Jessie

Reid (1991) draws a distinction between two kinds of knowledge about language: systematic knowledge and intuitive knowledge. She emphasises the importance of both kinds. Genre theory is not about formulaic teaching of language but rather about teaching basic ways of organising writing for different purposes. Children then have knowledge of how to organise meanings which they can manipulate as they imagine, explain, describe, instruct, etc.

There are structures in English; there is appropriate language. It is our professional judgement as to how far we teach this knowledge but it is also our professional responsibility to give children a critical understanding of the way in which our society uses language.

In Australia the genre debate became a political issue. In this country, the teaching of language is already a political issue. It may well be that genre ideas hold the key to bridging the gap between the notions of politicians and the informed practice of teachers.

References

BARRS, M. Genre theory. What's it all about? *Language Matters*, No.1. 1991-92. Centre for Language in Primary Education.

BRITTON, J., BURGESS, T., MARTIN N., MCLEOD, A., ROSEN, H. (1975). *The Development of Writing Abilities*, London: Macmillan.

CAMBOURNE, B. AND BROWN, H. (1989). Learning to Control different registers. In Andrews, R. (Ed) *Narrative and Argument*, Milton Keynes: Open University Press

CARTER, R. (Ed) (1990) *Knowledge about Language in the Curriculum: The LINC Reader*. London: Hodder & Stoughton

CHAPMAN, L.J. (1987) *Reading: From 5-11 years*. Milton Keynes: Open University Press

DEPARTMENT OF EDUCATION AND SCIENCE (1975) *A Language for Life*. London: HMSO

DEPARTMENT OF EDUCATION AND SCIENCE (1988) *Report of the Committee of Inquiry into the Teaching of English*. London: HMSO

DEPARTMENT OF EDUCATION AND SCIENCE (1989) *English for ages 5 to*

16. Proposals of the Secretary of State for Education and Science and the Secretary of State for Wales. London: HMSO

DEPARTMENT OF EDUCATION AND SCIENCE (1989) *English in the National Curriculum.* London: HMSO

DIXON, J. AND STRATTA, L. (1993) New demands in the model for writing in education - what does genre theory offer? In Heyhoe, M., & Parker, S. (Eds) *Reassessing Language and Literacy.* Milton Keynes: Open University Press

DONALDSON, M. (1988) *Sense and Sensibility.* Occasional Paper No.3. University of Reading, Reading and Language Information Centre

GRAVES, D. (1983) *Writing: Teachers and Children at Work.* London: Heinemann Educational.

HALLIDAY, M.A.K. AND HASAN, R. (1989) *Language, context, and text: aspects of language in a social-semiotic perspective.* Oxford: Oxford University Press.

HASAN, R. (1978) Text in the systemic-functional model. In Dressler, W.V., (Ed) *Current Trends in Text Linguistics.* New York: de Gruyter.

KRESS, G. (1989) Texture and Meaning. In Andrews, R. (ed) *Narrative and Argument.* Milton Keynes: Open University Press.

LITTLEFAIR, A.B. (1991) *Reading All Types of Writing.* Milton Keynes: Open University Press

MOFFET, J. (1968) *Teaching the Universe of Discourse.* Boston: Houghton Mifflin.

REID, J. Letter to *Language and Literacy News,* No.4. Spring 1991. United Kingdom Reading Association.

SHEERAN, Y. AND BARNES, D. (1991) *School Writing.* Milton Keynes: Open University Press.

WILKINSON, A., BARNSLEY, G., HANNA, P., SWAN, M. (1980) *Assessing Language Development.* Oxford: Oxford University Press.

Texts for Reading Assessment

Joyce M. Morris

During the last ten years or so the 'real books philosophy' has permeated infant school practice, teacher-training and published resources for developing initial literacy. Consequently, it is not surprising that, in line with National Curriculum documentation, 'trade' texts and informal assessment procedures formed the basis of Key Stage 1 Reading SATs in 1991. Moreover, as expected in an educational context characterised by heated controversy, SEAC responded to criticisms of those SATs mainly by introducing changes for 1992 which would have a minimal disruptive effect on what teachers had previously been asked to do and, hence, were unlikely to affect their morale.

Teachers' reactions to the 1992 SATs

The changes notably include two for Level 2, i.e. the Level which 'average' seven year olds could be expected to achieve. First, as accurate word recognition is an essential basic skill, this must now be assessed, albeit in a story context, and an accuracy grade given below which an award of Level 2 should be reconsidered. Second, for the 1992 assessments, teachers were advised to choose from only 14 books instead of 27 the previous year, and all of them had 'difficulty' scores within the same range having conformed to comparability criteria which included the use of *Spache Readability Formulae* and *Dale's 769 Word List*.

Despite the carefully-considered changes, to my knowledge, many heads and class teachers responsible for Key Stage 1 English were still not happy with how reading had to be legally assessed in 1992. They were not a representative sample taking part in a research project. Most of them contacted me primarily about prospects for a reprint edition of *Language in Action* which they valued as a uniquely-structured scheme incorporating *PHONICS 44* in story books by children's writers. Their effective use of that research-based, linguistics-informed scheme naturally contributed to their frequently-expressed view that it was better suited to integrating the teaching and assessment of reading than SATs using a miscellaneous selection of trade books by children's writers. It probably also influenced their judgement, or at least reflected the kind of teachers they are, that they were particularly pleased that the 1992 SATs included assessment of accurate word recognition but, nevertheless, felt that this aspect of reading is better assessed conventionally by means of standardized tests.

Be that as it may, the heads and class teachers were keen for me, as an independent researcher, to find out whether they were justified in being concerned about certain aspects of the 1992 Key Stage 1 Reading SATs, and the only way to do this was to carry out several kinds of text and word analysis. However, before doing so, I conferred with representatives of SEAC and the National Foundation for Educational Research (more precisely, the NFER Consortium) which had been commissioned to devise those SATs. They readily provided all the background information I needed from both organisations, including an internal, 'not-to-be-quoted', project paper which gives valuable insights into the scope of the SEAC brief and the difficulties encountered in its execution. In short, I was encouraged on all sides to proceed with my project since it concerned important issues raised at the chalkface, and would add a new dimension to the debate about reading assessment.

Level 2 texts for reading assessment

Because there is evidently most concern about the 1992 SATs for Reading Level 2, this paper focuses on them and, in particular, on the assessments of children's accuracy in word recognition whilst reading aloud. That is, the assessments which are the source of the greatest anxiety, at least among the teachers consulting me because, amongst other things, they include the possibility of 'demoting' otherwise 'average' seven year olds to 'below-average' Reading Level 1.

A useful starting point for my project report is the En2 Accuracy Grade Table from page 13 of the *Standard Assessment Task Teachers Handbook* for Key Stage 1 (HMSO, 1992). As can be seen (Table 1), it lists the titles of the 14 selected books for Level 2 with their respective Codes for recording purposes and, alongside the accuracy grades, gives the Check Scores below which teachers are required to reconsider an award of Level 2.

According to the Reference Notes for the 1992 SATs (SEAC October 1991) the 14 selected books 'have been carefully evaluated so that, although they vary in subject matter and presentation, they are comparable for assessment purposes. The factors taken into account in establishing comparability are: familiarity of vocabulary; sentence length; line length; cues from illustrations; repetition or rhythm; and the positioning of the assessed passage within the book. These factors interact in different ways in different passages, but overall comparability has been established'.

It would seem from the above statement that the NFER Consortium researchers commissioned by SEAC to devise the SATs were reasonably confident that the texts for reading assessment at Level 2 are of comparable difficulty. However, the teachers contacting me were not convinced that this is so, and their questions led me to look more closely at some of the factors taken into account by the research team, and other factors not within the scope of the SEAC brief and the timescale for its execution.

Table 1: En2 Accuracy Grade Table

Book	Code	Accuracy Grades					Check Score
		A	B	C	D	E	Scores below
			Number of marked words correct				this: reconsider
							award of level 2
Andrew's Bath	AB	25	23-24	21-22	19-20	up to 18	16
All in One Piece	AI	25	23-24	21-22	16-20	up to 15	8
But Martin!	BM	25	23-24	20-22	17-19	up to 16	12
The Bad-Tempered Ladybird	BT	25	23-24	20-22	16-19	up to 15	9
"Tomorrow" from Days with Frog and Toad	DF	25	24	22-23	17-21	up to 16	11
Dogger	DO	25	23-24	21-22	18-20	up to 17	14
"The Story" from Frog and Toad are Friends'	FF	25	23-24	21-22	18-20	up to 17	14
"A List" from Frog and Toad Together	FT	25	24	22-23	20-21	up to 19	16
Miss Dose the Doctors' Daughter	MD	25	24	23	22	up to 21	20
Mr and Mrs Hay the Horse	MH	25	23-24	21-22	19-20	up to 18	16
Mrs Wobble the Waitress	MW	25	24	23-24	18-21	up to 17	15
New Clothes for Alex	NC	25	23-24	21-22	18-20	up to 17	15
Peepo!	PE	25	23-24	21-22	18-20	up to 17	13
Whatever Next!	WN	25	23-24	21-22	18-20	up to 17	15

The basic question most frequently asked by the teachers was whether it mattered which book they chose for the reading assessment tasks, especially with regard to the passages selected by the research team for oral reading and the assessment of accuracy in word recognition. Accordingly, I first studied each book to find out what assistance the illustrations and the text offer the young reader in terms of picture and context cues to word recognition and meaning. I then noted, not surprisingly, that my findings were similar from more detailed analyses of the selected passages.

Briefly, these initial findings suggest that with regard to picture cues it would be advantageous for their pupils' assessments if teachers chose *Miss Dose the Doctor's Daughter* rather than, for example, 'A List' from *Frog and Toad Together*. Regarding the amount of contextual help given by repetition and rhythm for recognising and understanding difficult words and phases, *The Bad Tempered Ladybird* would be a good choice for a child not troubled by a variety of print sizes, sentence lengths, and rather frightening images. In other words the selected book which clearly exemplifies what the research team means by comparability assessment factors which 'interact in different ways in different passages' and, of course, in different books.

Words in context for reading assessment

In each selected passage, 25 words were chosen by the research team for the teachers' task of awarding grades for the children's accuracy in word recognition as shown in the EN2 Accuracy Grade Table (Table 1). How this was done is explained in the Reference Notes (SEAC, October 1991) as follows:-
'In order to identify the 25 words, the running record sheets from a sample of pupils who took part in the 1991 SAT were analysed. The difficulty of each word in the context of the passage was found from the proportion of children making errors. The words selected were those which gave the highest reliability to the assessment as a whole and gave a range of scores for the accuracy scale. Repetitions and proper names were excluded. The raw scores corresponding to each grade were also derived from these data. The grades correspond approximately to 20% bands of children within level 2'.

As will be seen, the above statement makes no reference to characteristics of the 350 selected words considered either as a total sample or individually for intrinsic difficulty. Consequently, it was the teachers' questions about them for which my analyses mainly sought answers.

Word frequency

First of all I analysed the total sample for word frequency. This was to get some idea of the chances of seven-year-olds being assessed for accuracy in word recognition on the same words as their peers as, conventionally, they could have been by means of a Standardized Word Recognition Test. The results showed that 82.46% of the 350 words had been chosen for the assessment only once, 14.03% twice, 2.81% three times, 0.35% four times and 0.35% seven times. Therefore, the chances of children being assessed on the same words as their peers, except of course if they read the same book, were poor to say the least.

At this point it must be stressed that this 'unfavourable' result and others reported below should not be interpreted as a criticism of the SATs' devisers. As already indicated, they worked to a timescale and a brief from SEAC which was not only in line with the National Curriculum for English Stage 1 but did not offer scope for the kind of analyses I was able to undertake.

Initial letters of words

Owing largely to the influence of the 'real books philosophy', the guessing of words from a story context and from their initial letters has been increasingly encouraged among infants in recent years. Understandably, this practice continues to cause heated debate, and prompted teachers, critical of the much-publicised theory of reading as a 'psycholinguistic guessing game', to ask questions about the Word Recognition SAT with regard to alphabet letters in initial word position.

Findings from the analysis I carried out to answer their questions indicated the presence of another significant chance factor in the Word Recognition SAT. This is exemplified by the fact that, of the 294 different selected words (as opposed to 350 instances), 31 begin with a capital letter and none of them with Qq, Xx or Zz. Moreover, the total frequency of instances for each letter (capital plus lower case) in initial word position ranges from 1 (u) to 41 (Tt). Thus for children with incomplete alphabet knowledge, their degree of success in accurately guessing the selected words would depend on which passage they were asked to read.

Words with punctuation

Because the SAT for accuracy in word recognition is based on words in story context, teachers were also worried about the effect of punctuation on the perceptual image of some selected words. I therefore analysed the texts for this variable and found that the image of 25.71% of the selected words is distorted to some degree by punctuation. Moreover, the range of words with punctuation is from 3 to 11, making *All in One Piece* the poorest choice with regard to this variable. Furthermore, as that book has the lowest check score (8) in the En2 Accuracy Grade Table, it is reasonable to suppose that the 'punctuation variable' contributed to the comparative difficulty of its selected words.

Types of words according to *Phonics 44*

The criteria for the selection of words did not take account of their intrinsic difficulty although the factor 'familiarity of vocabulary' was accounted for using *Dale's 769 Word List* as part of the *Spache Readability Formula*. As yet, no published details about that factor are available, but my analysis shows that 65.31% of the chosen words are on that List and, of the rest, only 2.04% are 'unfamiliar' according to the criteria established by NFER Consortium researchers.

I carried out further analyses 'book by book' because teachers suspected that the 25 selected words in each text are not of comparable, intrinsic difficulty and, hence, it mattered which selected passage they chose for the Word Recognition SAT. The first analysis focused on the number of syllables in each word as an indicator of word recognition difficulty. The second concentrated on the regularity, or otherwise, of sound-symbol correspondence according to *Phonics 44*; that is, my research-based linguistics-informed system for developing initial literacy in English (Morris, 1984) as incorporated, and used as a reference resource for this project, in *The Morris-Montessori Word List* (Morris, 1990).

Results from both analyses were then combined in Table 2 below to show how the 25 selected words in each book compare with regard to syllabic type and spelling regularity.

Table 2: Type of words according to *Phonics 44*

Books (Codes)	Word type (Number of Syllables and Regularity: R or I)										
	1		**2**		**3**		**4**		**Total**		**Total**
	R	I	R	I	R	I	R	I	R	I	words
AB	9	6	4	4	1	1	0	0	14	11	25
AI	11	5	4	5	0	0	0	0	15	10	25
BM	13	2	6	4	0	0	0	0	19	6	25
BT	10	5	6	2	0	2	0	0	16	9	25
DF	14	4	4	2	0	1	0	0	18	7	25
DO	7	4	10	3	0	1	0	0	17	8	25
FF	14	4	2	5	0	0	0	0	16	9	25
FT	11	9	1	4	0	0	0	0	12	13	25
MD	9	4	7	4	0	0	1	0	17	8	25
MH	8	4	7	2	2	1	1	0	18	7	25
MW	9	6	3	4	2	1	0	0	14	11	25
NC	7	9	4	4	0	1	0	0	11	14	25
PE	13	2	6	4	0	0	0	0	19	6	25
WN	7	7	4	4	2	1	0	0	13	12	25
Total											
No.	142	71	68	51	7	9	2	0	219	131	350
%	40.57	20.29	19.43	14.57	2.00	2.57	0.57	0	62.57	37.43	100

As can be seen, there are interesting differences between the books for both variables. These indicate that the teachers who contacted me were justified in suspecting that the selected words in each book are not of comparable difficulty. At the same time, the differences provide another illustration of the 'interaction' of variables to which the NFER Consortium researchers made reference, albeit with regard to different comparability factors from the two considered here.

For example, considering 'syllabic type' which is generally synonymous with word length and relative difficulty, 13 of the selected words in *Dogger* have two syllables whereas only 5 of them are disyllabic in 'A List' from *Frog and Toad Together*. Considering the second variable 'spelling regularity', like *Miss Dose the Doctor's Daughter*, previously mentioned for its supportive pictorial cues to word recognition, *Dogger* has only 8 selected words classed as 'irregular' compared with 13 in 'A List'.

For the total word sample, the percentages of words with one, two, three and four syllables are, respectively, 60.86%, 34%, 4.57% and 0.57%. Therefore, with regard to syllabic type, it represents proportionately the type of words which one would reasonably expect 'average' seven-year-olds to be able to read. Paradoxically, when one considers the results of analysing the total word sample for spelling regularity, there is a disproportionate percentage of 'irregular' words, i.e., 37.43% compared with the less than 10% found from orthographic research on which, for instance, *Phonics 44* is based. In other words, the comparatively low proportion in the English writing system exemplified by the comparatively few irregular words in The Morris-Montessori Word List (Morris, 1990).

Relationships between assessments of word difficulty

Returning to the basic question of whether it matters which book is chosen for a child's Word Recognition SAT, I ranked the books for the intrinsic difficulty of the selected words in each according to *Phonics 44*, and used the number of 'irregular' words shown in Table 2 as the criterion of difficulty. I then ranked the books for the difficulty of words in the context of the selected passages using the Check Scores in Table 1 as the criterion of difficulty.

On rational grounds this was a valid procedure insofar as the Check Scores indicate the number of errors in word recognition a child can make before being reconsidered for an award of Level 2. Thus, the lowest Check Score of 8 alongside *All in One Piece* was taken to mean that its word sample is the hardest and, therefore, that book was given the top difficulty rank (1). In contrast, with the highest Check Score of 20, *Miss Dose the Doctor's Daughter* has the easiest word sample and, accordingly, the lowest difficulty rank (14).

In practical terms, and bearing in mind the different criteria for word difficulty, the results of the ranking exercise could be interpreted as meaning that the chances of seven-year-olds not being demoted from Level 2 to Level 1 could be increased by their teacher's choice of book for their Word Recognition SAT. For instance, in this respect, they would be fortunate if asked to read the selected passage from *Miss Dose the Doctor's Daughter* especially as, as already stated, the artist provides comparatively good pictorial cues. *Mr. & Mrs. Hay the Horse* would also be a fortunate choice because it is highly ranked according to both kinds of difficulty criteria. Moreover, the best choice as far as the intrinsic difficulty of words is concerned would be *Peepo* or *But Martin* which are jointly ranked the easiest for this variable.

Conclusion

Considered together the results of the various analyses reported in this paper reveal that chance factors play too great a part in the Reading SATs for Level 2. They also highlight the complexities and dangers of using miscellaneous 'trade' texts for reading assessment especially when it is a question of accuracy in word recognition. In doing so, a new dimension is added to a good deal of previously accumulated evidence that the Reading SATs for seven-year-olds need to be reconsidered in order to make them more reliable and meaningful for all concerned with reading standards and the diagnosis of reading problems. In particular, the potential role of conventional standardized tests needs to be explored, and the technological expertise in this area fully utilised.

All this means of course that the National Curriculum for English Stage 1 should be reconsidered first or, at least, in conjunction with the SATs for 1993. Clearly, important changes are necessary to allow the teaching and assessment of reading to be brought in line with 'real knowledge' from professional research of various kinds and not, as hitherto, be subject to the undue influence of the 'real books philosophy'.

References

MORRIS, J.M. (1984) *Phonics 44* for initial literacy in English. *Reading* 18 (1) 13-24

MORRIS, J.M. (1990) *The Morris-Montessori Word List*. London Montessori Centre, 18 Balderton Street, London W.1

Children's Knowledge about Writing for Different Purposes: Planning for Progress

Pamela Owen

Introduction: becoming an independent writer

By the age of nine or ten, nearly all children show considerable competence in spoken English. Ability to give a simple account of their own personal experience is typically well established. Children can usually give a detailed oral account of an event; and often the account they give is well organised and sustained. Almost invariably, they can provide a rudimentary setting; they can say what they did; and they can tell you how things turned out. If the children can write down the words they need, transfer to the written mode might therefore seem straightforward. But there are crucial differences between speech and writing. In speech, children create texts in collaboration with their listeners who act as collaborative partners. The listeners provide prompts. They clarify obscurities of setting, reference and sequence. They also give continuous second-by-second feedback involving eye contact, posture and facial expression. Writing lacks this support.

The differences between speech and writing are reflected in the National Curriculum Statements of Attainment. From Level Four onwards the requirements for writing repeatedly include the word "independently". "Independence" is indeed an essential requirement for progress in writing. In the National Curriculum children are required to produce different types of extended writing. Progression is evident in both narrative and non-narrative forms. For non-narrative writing children are expected to move from simple lists to sophisticated analyses, and for narrative from simple personal accounts of what they did to fully developed narration involving plot, character and manipulation of time.

A glance at the problems

Example One: a 13 year-old's instructions to a friend on how to decorate a float for a festival.

"... then get the decorations like tinsel, tissue paper cardboard different colours and cut them in pieces and stick them on the lorry with drawing pins and then cut some more card."

This demonstrates two common weaknesses in instructional writing: failure to clarify by reference to positional markers; and inadequate separation of individual instructions.

Example Two: a 14 year old's story on the theme "From riches to rags" based on a picture of a dishevelled man playing a violin.

"The man started to gamble. His wife did not like it But he didn't understand he just kept on buying her gifts. After a while his wife left him with the kids. He got very depressed and went on the drink."

This extract reveals the flavour of the whole text in that it fails to provide details of feelings and presents events in the form of a list rather than expand them into episodes. The whole text reads like an objective account or report leaving the reader with little opportunity to empathise with the characters.

Example Three: A 14 year old's description of the style of clothing of one particular teenage group.

"She had a short denim skirt and a floppy teashirt with a picture of mickey mouse on. Her hair was unkempt and wild. It was a cold day and her legs were purple and goose pimpled. In one ear she had an earring the size of a bangle."

There is little attempt at organisation here, the writer simply making reference to one aspect after another and failing to integrated the whole.

Example Four: A 16 year old's essay on the value of a college cafeteria system.

"Our college canteen offers a very good range of food, it caters for everyone, from the health freak down to the egg and chips person. It's a shame that its the price that's putting people off. What a waste of food!"

The student describes a particular situation rather than use the situation to illustrate a point. There is also a tendency to veer away from the subject and a failure to consider alternative viewpoints.

To develop communicative competence in writing we need to free children from their dependence on conversational partners. We need to ensure that the system they internalise for generating and monitoring written discourse provides them with feedback to replace that of conversational interaction. Research at Manchester University into children's achievements in writing for different audiences and purposes suggests possible strategies for achieving feedback to replace conversational interaction.

The culmination of several years investigation into how children write for different audiences and purposes is a genre-based framework for monitoring progress and providing formative feedback. This teaching framework is central to the Joint Matriculation Board's Staged Assessments in Literacy (SAIL). SAIL has been used for some years to assess progress in writing at key stages 3 and 4 and has recently been employed very successfully to teach writing to primary children in years 5 and 6.

"Progression" and "formative feedback" are the two central features of the SAIL approach. In all aspects of writing children pass through discernible stages in the acquisition of competence. If we are to help them make progress in writing we need to specify "where children are at" and we need to identify teaching which will elicit progress. Often what is most important is getting children to understand precisely what it is they need to do. Mere acquaintance with the appropriate form of communication is insufficient. Children need to be provided with straightforward strategies which will enable them to achieve the desired effects the communication requires.

The writing framework provides coverage of all the types of extended writing included in the different subject demands of the National Curriculum.

Several assumptions underpin SAIL. The first is that progress in writing can be defined by reference to a functional model of language. Knowledge about writing is seen to be genre-bound.

Knowledge about writing

It is now widely recognised that language competence is relational to its context of use. Recognition of audience and purpose is a prerequisite for effective communication. This has led to increased attention being paid to the notion of genre. That genre and its importance in the teaching of English is now a hotly debated issue in English education circles, is largely due to the way in which Michael Halliday has untiringly draw the attention of linguists to the need to link the structures of language to their functional application. However, a little referenced source is that of Freidrich Schleiermacher (1819/1977) who was the one who extended the notion of context to encompass written forms of language. For the immediate environment of the spoken word is substituted the universe of written discourse within which various types of writing can be described.

Although there can be no tight specification of genre form, text structures are clearly not arbitrary designs. They arise from particular conventionalised social situations (Kress, 1981). What defines progress in writing? Is it patterns of use or accuracy of expression or both? More importantly, how can the various progress indicators be translated into teaching/learning objectives?

Regardless of the writing task, any writer is faced with three basic decisions. (i) what content to include; (ii) how to deploy the content and (iii) how to structure the content.

Selection of information determines the focus of the writing and establishes an appropriate relationship between writer and reader or audience. Whatever type of audience is perceived, the writer needs to adopt a complementary stance. This "Focus" dimension in the SAIL scheme corresponds closely with Jakobson's, (1960) model of discourse and the way in which texts are differentiated by theorists such as Kinneavy (1971) and Lloyd-Jones (1977) by reference to the "communicative triangle" establishing whether in the choice of information stress is placed on the writer, the reader or on the subject matter.

In the deployment of information the dimension of choice is that of the "Use" of information. This dimension features in a number of writing models being variously called "aims" (Kinneavy, 1971); "functions" (Jacobson, 1960, Britton, 1975); "force" (Brewer, 1980) and "forms" (Moffett, 1968). Essentially writers decide whether the dominant use of information will be characterised by specific descriptive statement, by expansion using reasons, examples or illustration or by comparative evaluation and examination.

The final dimension of choice concerns the "Organisation" of information. The different principles of organising texts have been described by Wilkinson (1986) as "primary acts of mind". Theorists either have a bipartite division into chronological and non-chronological (e.g. Perera, 1984); or a tripartite division (e.g. Kress, 1982) in which non-chronological writing is sub-divided into static, such as factual description and dynamic, such as persuasive writing.

The second assumption is that knowledge about writing should be explicitly taught.

Planning for progress: it all hinges on intervention

In SAIL, there are the elements of a framework or model of writing development which can be used to identify the constraining elements of different writing contexts and which can be used by the teacher as a device for planning children's progress.

Progress in writing competence can be described by reference to the degree of sophistication in the selection, use and organisation of information at the various "levels" of text. Audience, purpose and structural orientation define the context of the communication and influence the writer's linguistic choices. At the top or global level, progress is recognised through rhetorical form and at the local, intersentential level through variety and selectivity in the use of cohesive devices. At the word and sentence levels, accuracy and complexity of syntactic and word structures are the indicators of growth.

The teacher intervenes in the learning process by providing (i) opportunities for growth - task setting; (ii) a repertoire of strategies for achieving the desired effects - teaching objectives; (iii) feedback to show where expansion or greater explicitness is required through the collaborative reading of first drafts - assessment criteria; and (iv) shared knowledge about writing which enables negotiation about what has been achieved and what still needs to be worked on - records of achievement.

The setting of writing tasks is thus not a haphazard affair or a case of thinking simply, "Now what shall I ask them to write about to-day?" but a matter of careful task design. The requirements of the task need to be made explicit to pupils so they can make informed selections from their repertoire of writing strategies, monitor the effectiveness of their text as they write and read through first drafts purposefully.

Attempts have been made to identify text type structures schematically by mapping linguistic features on to the dimensions of discourse at the four "levels" of text. The principle followed has been to position features within a dimension on the basis of their functional role within the text. The knowledge about language which children require for this is encapsulated in the framework.

Within these broad choices as to the appropriate form of response to a writing task, pupils need to know the strategies to use to instantiate these decisions to produce fully formed coherent discourse of an appropriate type. They need in fact to know the "primary traits" (Lloyd- Jones, 1977) of the various discourse forms they are required to produce. These then act as a checklist for teachers and the pupils themselves when assessing achievement. Thus the notion of a single mark scheme regardless of writing task is rejected. The mark scheme is writing type specific. In this way pupils are able to receive targeted feedback directly relating to the teaching and learning objectives the task was designed to promote.

The third assumption is that complexity in writing is a function of the complexity of the writing task and that tasks can be graded.

Staging writing tasks

There are fourteen "types" of writing in SAIL. These reflect the purposes for writing identified by teachers. The staging of demand is based on a single variation on a concrete/abstract continuum. Task features are matched against context features and a score assigned on the basis of degree of abstractness. Each writing purpose allocated a profile score by reference to the communicative framework is positioned within a hierarchy of six stages according to perceived complexity. The scaling of task difficulty by writing type is represented as Figure 1.

Figure 1
Staging writing tasks

FOCUS	USE	ORGANISATION
Writer	Describe	Time
Subject	Expand	Group
Reader	Examine	Theme

From Figure 1, writing from personal experience with a descriptive aim while presenting information as a chronology of events is the easiest form of narrative writing and presenting a personal viewpoint with an expressive aim arranged around certain key points is an elementary form of exposition. These forms can be built up in terms of increasingly sophisticated writing types reaching fully formed reflective narration and analysis. Such "forms" are designed as stages in the acquisition of literacy - a means of building new knowledge on old.

The ordering of the writing types is designed to facilitate learning. As pupils work through the apprenticeship scheme their attention is focussed on particular strategies within each type of writing. The teaching aim is to assist pupils in building up a repertoire of strategies serving a range of purposes which as independent writers they will be able to deploy at will as appropriate to the genre form.

Children's achievements

The data reported below are drawn from assessment results over the period 1989 - 1992. Written responses for each writing "type" are assessed by reference to between 19 and 21 indicators of achievement. Each indicator is itself described by between 3 and 5 coded descriptors representing degree of achievement. Feedback to teachers and schools is by reference to statements of achievement allocated or not on the basis of a profile of performance across grouped indicators.

Analysis of the scores over the 4/5 years reveals the following findings.

Table One
Areas of greatest difficulty with KS2 writing types

Personal Account	Objective Report	Imaginative Account
A sense of occasion	Representing events	Expanding information
Personal comment	Specified outcome	Organisation
Syntax	Temporal sequence	Given/new
Punctuation	Temporal markers	Syntax
Word choice	Tense Word	Choice

Table Two
Areas of greatest difficulty with KS3 writing types

Information	Opinion	Narrative
Organisation	Justification	Reader interest
Objective stance	Cause & effect	Internal events
Topic sentences	Elaboration	Plot development
Connectives	Punctuation	Characterisation
Punctuation	Spelling	Syntax

Table Three
Areas of greatest difficulty with KS4 writing types

Persuasion	Reflection	Analysis
Expanding information	Evaluations	Examining information
Appeals	Organisation	Comparative evidence
Causality	Introspection	Cohesive ties
Paragraphs	Comparatives	Punctuation
Syntax	Syntax	Word choice

Table Four
Dimensions of difficulty in narrative writing

Audience (Focus)	-	capturing interest through plot and character
Purpose (Use)	-	expanding and examining information
Structure (Organisation)	-	none
Accuracy	-	syntax and local coherence

Table Five
Dimensions of difficulty in expository writing

Audience	-	maintaining objectivity
Purpose	-	detailing information about characteristic features
Structure	-	forming categories
Accuracy	-	markers of relative position and paragraph structure

These findings are not surprising. They simply make explicit what teachers realise to be the particular demands of different written genres. There is relatively little difficulty with organising narrative forms but there is difficulty in both the expansion of information and in producing the complex syntactic forms such expansion requires. In expository writing, organising information is a fundamental difficulty which is realised in both semantic and syntactic inaccuracies of paragraphing.

The fourth assumption of the SAIL scheme is that systematic TA is the key to raising standards of literacy.

Classroom application

The first example is a response by a nine-year-old girl to a Personal Account task on the topic of "Conflict". The children were asked to write about a time when they had a big argument with someone. ("It might have been with one of your family, a shopkeeper or a friend at school.") They were asked to say what led up to the argument, what happened and how it all turned out.

Saraya's script
One day when I was in the Infants we were Just going Into school in the morning. When we were going up the stairs and I stepped on my freinds coat by accident. I said sorry but she didn't answer. When we whent Into the class she was with her best freind talking about the pretend money she had then I told her that my sister had that money and she didnt say anything so I felt bad. When we whent out to play I was going to play with my freind but they Just turnd away and gave me dirty looks so I just sat on the bench. In dinner play I sat on the bench again and I saw them all having fun and skiping. I was Just on the bench then a teacher came and asked me why I was on my own I said that they wernt my freind so she told them to be my freind but they didnt want to at first but then they were freinds again and I had a good time because when my freinds arnt my freinds and then we make up the treat you really good and let you in on everything. they make you feel like your the best thing thats why I like my freinds so much.

When matched against the statements of attainment for Level One Personal

63

Account, Saraya can be seen to have:
• recognised the task requirement to write a personal account
• provided information about personal activities
• related the activities to one main occasion
• covered a number of events
• ordered events in temporal sequence.

However,
• the activities amount to little more than a list
• there is little in the way of personal comment
• reference is insufficiently specific
• expression is often inaccurate.

Saraya needs time to consolidate these skills before tackling more advance forms of writing.

The second example is a response by a fourteen year old boy to a Persuasion task on the topic of "Keeping Fit". In both the rhetorical and expressive domains the pupil fulfils all the demands of this type of writing at Stage Five.

Letter to Vera

Dear Vera,

I hope you are feeling better but I am sad to hear of your current state of ill health. Your obesity must be a distressing part of your life. In my letter I will try to outline the advantages of exercise, how it has helped me and how it can help you.

As the weather improves my family and I are finding that our enjoyment of exercise and sport are increasing. The social advantages of participating in the sports that we do are immense and since beginning to exercise we have found ourselves invited out to far more social functions.

I know that you have found exercising and keep fit to have been distressing in your earlier life and can understand how your experiences of strict high school gym mistresses could make you dislike exercise but it need not be such an ordeal. Your love of dancing has always been in you and this activity could be the perfect way to get more fit. The ryhthmic movments will improve you heart and muscles of a long period as well as helping you to lose weight. Your arthritis could even be improved. It is important to know that exercise does not only consist of a regimen of press ups and touching you toes but can be enjoyed.

I myself enjoy swimming and I encourage you to take it up as I have found it benefits me immensely. The body is totally exercised in this sport as every muscle group is used at some time during it. The water itself is very soothing to the body and can even help cure tensness and improve stamina. Joining a local swimming club will help you keep fit and meet new people as well as learn a valuable new skill which if you teach it to yuour children could save someone's life; it is also great fun.

I recently heard about Uncle Arthur's death and distressing though it was we all know that his death was hastened by an unhealthy lifestyle. By the time of his death he was a pathetic wretched mass of fat and spent muscle, wasting away before his families eyes. Though it pains me to compare you to him I find that I must do so to inform you that it is not too late and that if you take action now you can improve your life.

If you start dancing again and take up swimming both can become enjoyable passtimes and will certainly contribute to keeping fit.

Finally I must leave you with the knowledge that all of us, yourself included hold the safety and welfare of our children in our hands and that it is you duty to instruct them how to lead a healthy life. Learning how to exercise and keep fit along with the benefits and enjoyment which come from doing so are amongst the greatest gifts we can give to out children.

For all our sakes and for your health and happiness take some exercise.
Best Wishes

Commentary

There is a clear "focus" on a specified reader "Vera" throughout with attempts to influence her behaviour. For example,
"Learning how to exercise and keep fit along with the benefits and enjoyment which come from doing so are amongst the greatest gifts we can give to out children."

A number and range of different appeals are made to the reader:
• reference is made to what the writer has found of benefit,
"I myself enjoy swimming and I encourage you to take it up as I have found it benefits me immensely. The body is totally exercised in this sport as every muscle group is used at some time during it.";
• reference is made to the fate of a relative who did not keep fit,
" I recently heard about Uncle Arthur's death and distressing though it was we all know that his death was hastened by an unhealthy lifestyle.";
• reference is made to the reader's own likes,
"Your love of dancing has always been in you and this activity could be the perfect way to get more fit."

There are a number of other tactics used such as drawing attention to Vera's "arthritis", to the social advantages of taking up a sport and to a parent's duty to her children.

All the information is appropriately grouped with paragraph divisions made on the basis of the different appeals being made. Most paragraph divisions are marked by topic sentences and considerable use is made of causal and conditional semantic relations to link sentences and units of a sentence. For example,

" Though it pains me to compare you to him I find that I must do so to inform you that it is not too late and that if you take action now you can improve your life."

The way in which the reader is involved is marked by the extensive use of interpersonal reference with first and second person pronouns used throughout. For example,

" I must do so to inform you."

"I recently heard....we all know that..."

Markers of the hypothetical are also used as in "If you start dancing again...." and "if you teach it to your children..."

Expression is accurate throughout. Apart from an occasional lapse, complex sentences are well structured and punctuated and words with more complex structures such as "muscle" and "distressing" are correctly spelled. There has been a move away from concrete vocabulary and the humorous treatment of the topic is refreshing.

Conclusion

In writing, although texts are not normally collaborative, children cannot be left to their own devices. Independence in writing is not something which naturally emerges. It needs to be strategically planned. The teacher needs to act as a "collaborative partner" by helping the child to establish context by reference to the genre form to be produced. If the teacher is to support the child in a systematic and principled way some form of communicative framework is necessary so that children and teachers share a common language for talking about writing. The great advantage of SAIL is that it provides such a framework and enables the teacher to give feedback which is more than vague conferred recommendation. The child is able to perceive that success has been achieved rather than simply be told. In this way we can enable children to have continual experience of success as they make progress by achieving successive objectives and tackle increasingly more difficult writing tasks.

References

BEVERIDGE, M. (1991) Literacy Problems in Secondary Schools: Problems of Texts and Teaching, *Educational and Child Psychology* Vol. 8 No. 3

BREWER, W.F. (1980) 'Literacy, Theory, Rhetoric and Stylistics: Implications for Psychology' in R J Spiro et al (eds) *Theoretical Issues in Reading Comprehension*, New Jersey: Lawrence Erlbaum.

BRITTON, J et al (1975) *The Development of Writing Abilities 11-18*, Schools Council: MacMillan Press.

CHRISTIE, T et al (1989) A cross-curricular approach to language achievement: The JMB's Staged Assessments in Literacy, *Head Teachers' Review*, Spring.

DES/ WELSH OFFICE (1989) *English in the National Curriculum*, London: HMSO.

FLOWER, L & HAYES, J R (1984) The Dynamics of Composing: making plans and judging constraints, in LW Gregg and EP Steinberg (Eds) *Cognitive Processes in Writing*, New Jersey: Lawrence Erlbaum.

JAKOBSON, R. (1960) 'Linguistics and Poetics' in T A Sebeok, (Ed) *Style in Language*, New York: John Wiley & Sons.

JOINT MATRICULATION BOARD (1987) *The SAIL Handbook*, Manchester: JMB

KINNEAVY, J L (1971) *A Theory of Discourse*, Engelwood Cliffs, New Jersey: Prentice-Hall Inc.

MOFFETT, J (1968) *Teaching the Universe of Discourse*, Boston: Houghton Mifflin.

NFER (1992) *Writing Rescue*, Slough: NFER

LLOYD-JONES, R (1977) 'Primary Trait Scoring' in C R Cooper and L Odell (Eds) *Evaluating Writing*, Urbana, Illinois: NCTE

PERERA, K (1984) *Children's Writing and Reading; analysing classroom language*, Oxford: Basil Blackwell.

WILKINSON, A et al (1980) *Assessing Language Development*, Oxford: Oxford University Press.

WILKINSON, A (1986) *The Writing of writing*, Milton Keynes: Open University Press.

Comparative Text Processing in Expository Prose: Examining Textual Attributes in Print and Computer Mediated Presentation

Joseph D. Rivard

Text Structure.

The transition from narrative text to expository prose is difficult for many students. The organization of facts and conceptual ideas are arranged differently in informational materials. Expository text tends to classify data hierarchically, with larger conceptual ideas preceding more detailed factual content. The nature of expository material in content area textbooks requires the learner to delineate important information, extract main ideas, and create written reflective summaries and critiques. The nature of expository material in multi-media and computer mediated instructional formats requires many of the same tasks. Information must be located, comprehended, manipulated, and applied.

In conventional formats, learners struggle not only with the reading of expository prose, but the writing of it as well (Applebee, Langer, and Mullis, 1989). Well written expository reports and essays are achieved with great difficulty by many. In learning environments embellished with instructional technology, students must also craft expository prose which may accompany pictorial, graphic, and video information. Crafting such prose is once again a challenging endeavour.

Reasons why children struggle with exposition regardless of instructional format may include a lack of knowledge regarding the manner in which content area information is organized and structured. Thus, some would suggest we begin to solve this problem by teaching children about expository text structure.

Teaching Text Structure

In the typical print formats, teaching text structure may be accomplished through many diverse approaches. One strategy teaches readers to use textual cues as comprehension guides. Attention to outlines, headings, subheadings and font draw the reader purposefully to content. Other strategies expose children to the basic patterns inherent in expository text. Text patterns allow concept information and conceptual information to be linked together in order to foster content comprehension. Noting similarities and differences among facts and concepts, sequencing facts and concepts, and understanding how facts and concepts are caused by other facts and concepts are typical patterns used in expository material. When students identify these patterns and understand their function, learning may be facilitated with greater ease. Additional strategies encourage concrete conceptual mapping of text information.

In electronic formats, teaching text structure may be complicated by its generic disposition. In a conventional environment the learner is confronted with a text consisting of several hundreds of pages, defined by one topical domain. Within the text the content is subdivided by chapters. Each chapter may have 25-30 pages, and material therein is further subdivided into chapter sections of 3-5 pages. Teaching text structure within this format is challenging, but attainable. In multi-media environments the typical CD-ROM content disc holds over 500 million characters of information stored in digital format. Only one page is visible on screen at any given moment, and content is more broadly packaged than finely focused content area texts. The voluminous nature of electronic text therefore requires the teacher to re-examine methodological approaches to expository material. An understanding of any number of information handling skills must accompany the understanding of expository text structure. The ability to identify the kind of information needed to solve a problem in order to establish a "match" with the variety of data bases available becomes a prerequisite. Learning both how to locate and acquire information that has been identified electronically becomes an entirely new challenge (Mancall, Lodish, and Springer, 1992). Only after the information is located and acquired can the content be analyzed, synthesized, and applied in constructive ways.

For those who employ computer mediated instruction, a word of caution. Prior to exposing students to large electronic data bases, content discs, or electronic reference material, it may be helpful to teach text structure using foundational software. Some may choose to categorize foundational software programs by discourse classification (cause/effect, compare/contrast, sequencing, etc). It has been suggested that at least three types of foundational software programs may be used to help students learn text structure (Dowd and Sinatra, 1991). *Modelling software programs* display categories of text structure. These programs require the student to read and write according to modelled text styles. Students read electronic discourse, and then write discourse based upon the prototype model that was read. *Interactive software programs* contribute to the learning of text structure by allowing the students to dialogue with the computer. Learners contribute their own novel ideas in combination with electronic discourse in order to generate prose. *Desktop publishing programs* enable students to employ prior knowledge in combination with new knowledge gleaned from expository printed text. Functional prose is created for class newspapers, or desktop publishing projects which give meaning and relevance to the task.

Students must become familiar with text structure by reading expository material and writing expository prose successively in simplified software formats prior to exposure to more sophisticated electronic information sources. Dowd recommends *Thinking Networks for Reading and Writing, Creative Writer, Organize*, and *Writing Process Workshop* as fundamental tools which will assist the teacher in teaching text structure in technologically rich learner environments.

Advantages of Teaching Text Structure

Reading comprehension improves as knowledge of text structure increases (Taylor and Beach, 1984; Berkowitz, 1986; Piccolo, 1987). Understanding the inherent attributes of electronic or printed text increases the success with which students are able to comprehend and manipulate information. As improvement in reading comprehension correlates with knowledge of text structure, one might wonder if knowledge of text structure results in parallel improvement for writing expository prose. Many have demonstrated that instruction about text structure does improve both reading comprehension and expository writing (Shanahan, 1988; Raphael, Kirschner, and Englert, 1988).

Text Processing and Comprehensibility

Electronic expository instructional materials are now available in large quantity. Many educators have supplemented their learning environments with instructional technology supporting electronic text. The inclusion of multi-media and computer mediated instructional material provokes interest in the comprehensibility in both mediums. Do readers comprehend text better if it is displayed electronically or conventionally?

Studies have suggested that computer mediated expository passages do facilitate increased comprehension over printed text (Reinking and Schreiner, 1985; Anderson and Anderson, 1984). It would appear that computer mediated presentation offers the reader two comprehension advantages over text. Computer mediated text provides "help" options for the locating and defining of relational data, and slows down the rate of reading time (Reinking, 1988). In combination, these two events seem to provide electronic expository material certain comprehension advantages. Perennial to the discussion of comprehension advantage in computer mediated instruction is the extent to which individuals find the electronic medium more interesting than conventional printed text. If the medium is perceived as motivational, and the motivational locus does not dissipate with the absence of novelty, an additional comprehension advantage may be apparent as a result of increased attention (Hidi, 1991). As researchers explore the subtleties of information processing theory, we are beginning to appreciate the arousal contingent upon multi-modal sensory stimulation (Nejad, 1988). Performance increases in relation to the strength of arousal. Successively this increases our ability to maintain attention, fostering improved comprehension.

Conclusion

In view of contemporary cognitive perspectives, the linkages between prior knowledge, reading, writing, thinking, understanding, and the recognition of different text structures are substantial (Meyer, 1984). Textual patterns in expository material provide organizational frameworks for content. When these patterns are understood by the student, reading and writing are improved. Knowledge of structure facilitates thinking and understanding.

Indeed, textual comprehensibility involves more than vocabulary difficulty or sentence length (Beck, McKeowen, Sinatra, and Loxterman, 1991). As we find ourselves confronted with expository material in both electronic and conventional formats, it is more imperative than ever to initiate instruction on the nature of text structure. Educators need to remain sensitive to the attributes unique in each medium, and use each to its best advantage. Regardless of the books or bytes employed, each format must be utilized efficiently. After all, much of the knowledge of greatest worth comes from interaction with expository materials (McNeil, 1987).

References

ANDERSON, T., AND ANDERSON, R. (1984). An Experimental Evaluation of a Computer Based Study Management System. *Educational Psychologist*, 11, 189-190.

APPLEBEE, A., LANGER, J. AND MULLIS, I., (1989). *Crossroads in American Education*. Princeton, NJ: Educational Testing Service.

BECK, I., MCKEWON, M., SINATRA, G. AND LOXTERMAN, J. (1991). Revising Social Studies Text From a Text Processing Perspective: Evidence of Improved Comprehensibility. *Reading Research Quarterly* 26(3), 251-276.

BERKOWITZ, S. (1986). Effects of Instruction In Text Organization On Sixth Grade Students' Memory For Expository Reading. *Reading Research Quarterly*, 21, 161-168.

DOWD, C. AND SINATRA, R. (1990). Computer Programs and the Learning of Text Structure. *Journal of Reading*, 34(2), 104-112.

HIDI, S. (1991). Interest and its Contribution as a Mental Resource for Learning. *Review of Educational Research*, v.60(4)

MANCALL, J., LODISH, E., AND SPRINGER, J. (1992). Searching Across the Curriculum. *Kappan*, March, 526-528.

MCNEIL, J. (1987). *Reading Comprehension: New Directions for Classroom Practices, (2nd ed.).* Glenview, IL: Scott Foresman.

MEYER, B. (1984). Organizational Aspects of Text: Effects on Reading Comprehension and Applications for the Classroom. In J. Flood (ed.), *Handbook of Reading Research,* White Plains, NY: Longman.

NEJAD, A. (1987). Cognitive and Affective Causes of Interest and Liking. *Journal of Educational Psychology*, v.79(2).

PICCOLO, J. (1987). Expository Text Structure: Teaching and Learning Strategies. *The Reading Teacher*, 40, 838-847.

RAPHAEL, T., KIRSCHNER, B., AND ENGLERT, C. (1988). Expository Writing Program: Making Connections Between Reading and Writing. *The Reading Teacher*, 41, 790-795.

REINKING, D. (1988). Computer Mediated Text and Comprehension Differences: The Role of Reading Time, Reader Preference, and Estimation of Learning. *Reading Research Quarterly*, 23(4), 484-498.

REINKING, D. AND SCHREINER, R. (1985). The Effects of Computer Mediated Text On Measures of Reading Comprehension and Reading Behavior. *Reading Research Quarterly*, 20, 536-552.

SHANAHAN, T. (1988). The Reading-Writing Relationship: Seven Instructional Principles. *The Reading Teacher*, 41, 636-647.

TAYLOR, B., AND BEACH, R. (1984). The Effects of Text Structure Instruction on Middle Grade Students' Comprehension and Production of Expository Text. *Reading Research Quarterly*, 19, 134-146.

Developing Background Knowledge: A Context Enrichment Strategy that may Provide more Consistent Results than Activation of Prior Knowledge

Sara Brody

Many children aged 10 - 12 experience difficulty when trying to understand their textbooks. This problem seems to be particularly acute when science and social studies lessons present unfamiliar and specialized topics. Since children generally have the intellectual ability to understand new concepts (Chall, 1983; Inhelder & Piaget, 1958), what can be done to improve students' comprehension of unfamiliar text?

A variety of research projects, conducted with 10-12 year old children, provide evidence related to this issue. Several classroom studies have examined the effectiveness of the practice of "activating" prior knowledge (encouraging children to recall the knowledge they already possess before reading a text). Although results with this practice were mixed, activation of prior knowledge is often recommended as a means of making the reader's background more available to contribute to reading comprehension. Since the results of these studies are inconsistent, additional research has been conducted to clarify the role of prereading instruction in comprehension of a text. More recent studies suggest that prereading instruction designed to activate prior knowledge may be less effective than prereading instruction that directly provides children with accurate and relevant background before reading.

Why "activation" of prior knowledge was recommended

Theorists postulate that prior knowledge plays an important role in the comprehension of text. Reading comprehension theory suggests that comprehension occurs when a reader constructs a schema (an understanding of the text) by combining the information presented in a text with knowledge the reader already possesses (Perfetti & Curtis, 1986). Schema theory suggests that it is this interaction of what is in print and what is in the reader's mind that produces what is finally comprehended (understood or misunderstood). Researchers postulate that recalling what one knows concerning a topic, along with making conscious use of that knowledge, will lead readers to form a schema of the text more easily. Therefore, strategies designed to stimulate prior knowledge activation have often been recommended as a means of enhancing reading comprehension.

For example, if a text on farming in Switzerland were assigned, a teacher might probe to activate students' prior knowledge by asking students what they think people do to produce milk and milk products. Another approach teaches the strategy of consciously using one's knowledge to make sense of text when a difficult section is encountered during reading. For example, if a passage concerning Swiss grazing practices were confusing, students would be prompted to think about what they know about farming in general. They would be encouraged to use their knowledge as a context within which to interpret the confusing text.

Potential problems related to the strategy of activating prior knowledge to enhance comprehension

The knowledge readers possess before they begin to read is very powerful. People tend to remember and rely on what they already know when encountering new information. Even when readers' prior knowledge is inaccurate, it often overrides the accurate information read in a text (Wilson & Anderson, 1986; Lipson, 1984). For example, based on their inaccurate prior knowledge, readers may continue to think that whales are fish, not mammals, even after reading a text that explains that they are warm blooded, need to surface for air every 10 - 30 minutes, and nurse their young. Even though the text presents explanatory information, the reader's prior knowledge may still override what is in print. Consequently, it seems that the strategy of activating prior knowledge may inadvertently lead to a misunderstanding of text by refreshing readers' misconceptions before reading.

In prereading activities that encourage readers to recall their prior knowledge, teachers often ask students to discuss their thoughts and experiences related to a topic to be studied. The usefulness of information learned during these activities depends upon the accuracy and relevance of the prior knowledge that classmates share during prereading activation. For example, prereading instruction concerning a passage about whales may begin by asking students to tell their ideas about whales. If students indicate that whales are fish because they swim, this may reinforce misinformation or provide misinformation to students who knew nothing about whales. Even when readers work independently, if their knowledge concerning a topic under study is limited, recalling that knowledge may not offer a sufficiently rich context to support the reading of unfamiliar text. In short, strategies designed to activate the knowledge a reader already possesses before coming to a text may not compensate sufficiently for the limited or inaccurate knowledge that many young readers possess as they begin to read unfamiliar and specialized text.

Classroom studies of prior knowledge activation strategies

Several studies comparing activation strategies with other methods of instruction have been conducted with 10 - 12 year old children. One study (Hansen & Pearson, 1983) finds mixed results, sometimes favouring instruction that uses activation strategies, other times favouring instruction that briefly introduces the topic and several pertinent points. A review of the methods compared suggests that when the prior knowledge activation was more effective, the strategy also generally included an instructional element that conveyed some of the pertinent and central concepts of the text under study while the comparison approaches gave only cursory introduction to the topic.

A later study (Anstey & Freebody, 1987) found somewhat similar results. In this study, several approaches designed to activate prior knowledge were compared. One approach provided exposure, through a picture, to the central concept of a text before reading. In this approach, students wrote their ideas concerning the content of a passage while viewing a picture that depicted the main concept of the story. In two comparison approaches, no direct exposure to the central text concept was provided. Instead, students wrote free associations either from the story title or from questions related to the topic to be read. In this study, only the strategy of exposing the main story concept (with a picture) was related to an advantage over reading the passage without any prereading instruction. These findings suggest that students who studied the story related picture may have benefitted from exposure to pertinent concepts or information before the reading of unfamiliar text.

Two later studies (Brody, 1991; Dole, Valencia, Greer & Wardrop, 1991) explore further the questions raised by classroom comprehension studies. They examine whether it is the activation of prior knowledge or, instead, the teaching of pertinent and important background concepts that is related to enhanced comprehension of a text among 10 - 12 year olds. In these studies, a method that presents central background concepts and information is compared with an approach that asks students to recall knowledge that they already possess. These strategies are also compared with the reading of a passage after no prereading instruction at all. The results of both studies (Brody, 1991; Dole et al., 1991) indicate an advantage associated with the strategy of teaching background information related to the text under study when compared with either activation or with no prereading instruction at all. These studies lend further evidence suggesting that reading comprehension of an assigned text may be enhanced by developing relevant background knowledge and important concepts before reading. Further, they suggest that drawing out prior knowledge alone does not seem to be associated with enhanced comprehension of a passage.

Strategy for the Development of Background Knowledge

Instruction that develops background knowledge presents crucial concepts needed to understand the text (Brody, 1991). This is done in several steps. First, the teacher tells, reads, or demonstrates a concept or some information related to a text that students are about to read. (In preparing the presentation, the teacher may draw on a parallel text, encyclopedia, trade book, visual media or other resources.) Next, the teacher asks questions that lead students to explain and apply what they have learned from the teacher's presentation. When a student's response to a question is accurate, the teacher confirms the response and sometimes repeats it in similar words to reinforce the information for all the class. Alternatively, when a student's response to a question is inaccurate, the teacher says, "Actually, ..." and then explains the information again using other wording or perhaps a diagram or picture as well. In this case, the teacher would ask additional questions to assure that the clarifying explanation was understood. This process of first presenting a concept, then asking questions that require explanation and application, and finally confirming or reiterating the concept, is repeated several times. The number of concepts presented will vary with the background of the class. The teacher needs to present those concepts necessary to develop sufficient background knowledge to provide a rich context from which to read the text.

For example, students could be presented with an explanation of the concept "irrigation" by the teacher. Then they could be asked to tell how it is used to solve a problem, or how irrigation works, in order that they might actively apply the concept in their own words. If a student's answer indicates a misunderstanding of irrigation, the teacher would acknowledge the student's response by saying, "Actually, irrigation is used in this way..." The teacher then asks the same student the question again, in order to provide an opportunity for the student to experience success and in order to be sure that the teacher's revised explanation was understood.

Such a strategy can be used along with the materials and manuals that teachers already have in their classrooms. The only adjustment necessary is to begin by providing students with information concerning a concept and to follow with questions that encourage students to discuss the concept. This is in contrast to beginning as well as ending the prereading lesson by encouraging students to discuss a concept, without first receiving accurate information to use in developing thoughts and responses. The approach can be used in whole class, small group, or individual instruction. The crucial elements appear to be:
1) accurate presentation of relevant concepts by the teacher,
2) an opportunity for students to express their understanding of the concepts through the answering of questions that require an explanation and application of the concept, and
3) immediate confirmation or else clarification by the teacher if the student's response suggests a misunderstanding of the concept.

The appeal of prior knowledge activation strategies.

Educators want to provide opportunities for students to learn concepts and facts in contexts that allow information to be fully integrated and understood. Teachers are concerned that if students are presented with information, rather than encouraged to work at drawing from what they already know, the information will not be as useful or available for future application. Many teachers view activation of prior knowledge approaches as a means to involve students in thinking, discussion, and application of concepts before and during reading. However, the studies reviewed here indicate that the practice of prior knowledge activation alone does not seem to aid in comprehension of text among 10 - 12 year olds.

The positive attributes of integrating and applying concepts under study can be incorporated into the strategy of directly developing background knowledge if information is not only presented by the teacher but also actively processed by the students. Such processing can be stimulated by asking children to answer questions that encourage rethinking, applying, and restating the information in a related context. For example, students could be presented with an explanation of the concept "pollination" by the teacher. Then students could apply the concept in their own words by answering questions concerned with how farmers plant their crops to increase pollination. The offering of information by the teacher need not replace active involvement in learning; instead it can give students rich and accurate background knowledge to work with while developing and articulating their thoughts. Further, students may be able to use the information, while reading, to understand the text more clearly. Rather than coming to the process of constructing meaning with inaccurate background, students enter the process with a context of pertinent and enriched background.

Conclusions

Compatibility with schema theory.

Schema theory suggests that readers comprehend text by integrating what they read with what they know in order to construct a text schema. Studies conducted with 10 - 12 year old students suggest that an advantage is associated with prereading instruction that presents text related concepts in order to develop an enriched background of knowledge. This research seems to suggest that instruction that develops accurate and relevant background knowledge facilitates the forming of a meaningful text schema. This conforms with the findings of earlier studies which indicate that readers who possess accurate and relevant knowledge concerning a new text understand it better than those who possess inaccurate or tangential knowledge (Barnitz & Morgan, 1983; Lipson, 1984; Wilson & Anderson, 1986).

Instruction.

It appears that 10 - 12 year old children understand text better when it is approached from a context of knowing accurate and relevant background. Recent studies suggest that teachers can prepare students to read and learn about the unfamiliar by directly teaching and developing an accurate and relevant context for the topic before reading. This can be done by presenting and clarifying pertinent concepts before reading, rather than by asking students only to recall what they know concerning the unfamiliar or specialized topic. Teachers can adapt their lessons and manuals to include this strategy by teaching relevant concepts and background before carrying out discussion activities that ask students their thoughts about a topic before reading.

Further research.

There is a need for research to determine whether the findings presented here are applicable to older and younger students as well as to 10 - 12 year olds. Additional studies with 10 - 12 year olds are needed to provide evidence concerning the number of exposures and types of exposures to each concept that are needed to optimize learning from science and social studies texts. Additional research is needed to determine how best to integrate teacher instruction in pertinent concepts with active student application in order to maximize the richness, relevance, and accuracy of the context that students bring to text.

Summary.

Relevant background knowledge appears crucial to 10 - 12 year olds' understanding of unfamiliar and specialized text. We need to provide students with accurate information and concepts before they begin to read challenging text. In addition to presenting background knowledge and filling in gaps in prior knowledge, we need to provide opportunities for students to express their newly developing understanding in their own words. This can be done by posing questions that encourage students to reformulate and apply the relevant concepts and background that have been presented by the teacher. With such preparation, students may experience success when reading unfamiliar and specialized text and learn to view reading as an opportunity for constructively interacting with new concepts and ideas rather than as a dreaded exercise in frustration and misunderstanding.

References

ANSTEY, M.M. & FREEBODY, P. (1987). The effects of various pre-reading activities on children's literal and inferential comprehension. *Reading Psychology*, 8(3), 189-209.

BARNITZ, J.C. & MORGAN, A.L. (1983). Aspects of schemata and syntax in fifth grade children's inferential reading comprehension of causal relations. *Reading Psychology*, 4(3), 337-48.

BRODY, S. (1991). *Clarifying the role of prereading instruction in 4th graders' comprehension of social studies text.* Doctoral Dissertation, Harvard Graduate School of Education. Ann Arbor, Michigan: University Microfilms, Inc.

CHALL, J.S. (1983). *Stages of reading development.* New York: McGraw-Hill.

DOLE, J.A., VALENCIA, S.W., GREER, E.A., & WARDROP, J.L. (1991). Effects of two types of prereading instruction on the comprehension of narrative and expository text. *Reading Research Quarterly*, 26(2), 142-159.

HANSEN, J. & PEARSON, P.D. (1983). An instructional study: Improving the inferential comprehension of good and poor fourth-grade readers. *Journal of Educational Psychology*, 75(6), 821-29.

INHELDER, B. & PIAGET, J. (1958). *The growth of logical thinking from childhood to adolescence.* New York: Basic Books.

LIPSON, M.Y. (1984). Some unexpected issues in prior knowledge and comprehension. *Reading Teacher*, 37(8), 760-764.

PERFETTI, C.A. & CURTIS, M.E. (1986). Reading. In R.F. Dillon & R.J. Sternberg (Eds.), *Cognition and Instruction.* Academic Press.

WILSON, P.T. & ANDERSON, R.C. (1986). What they don't know will hurt them: The role of prior knowledge in comprehension. In J. Orasanu (Ed.), *Reading comprehension: From research to practice.* Hillsdale, NJ: Lawrence Erlbaum.

Learning from Text: Let's Get Practical

Marian J. Tonjes

There is indeed a plethora of reading, writing and learning strategies in today's literature. In fact, at times we may wonder which might be more productive to meet our aims. Help is on the way.

In the second edition of the Handbook of Reading Research, Pearson and Fielding (1991) discuss this very issue. What makes some strategies more effective than others? They point out that the more useful strategies have four characteristics. These can easily be recalled by using the acronym "**BUMS**". A good strategy they maintain will help readers to:

B   1.   Build Bridges - or connections between readers' knowledge and the text, or what readers already know will serve as a background or foundation for the new knowledge to be gained.

U   2.   Use Knowledge of text structures - perceiving types of text such as expository, narrative, perceiving paragraph organisation (e.g. compare/contrast, definition, summary), in other words, how this text material is put together - its genre.

M   3.   Monitor for Meaning - here is where metacognition really plays a part with the readers being able to stay aware of whether they are comprehending appropriately and, if not, knowing what to do, what fix-up strategy to use.

S   4.   Summarize - doing this automatically decreases the problem of loose items floating around unattached, unconnected to main points.

So, the more effective strategies should help to build bridges, use text structures, monitor for meaning and automatically summarize.

Let us look now at some of the current or popular strategies to see which best fit this BUMS model.

Strategy 1: Response Journals

Students record in notebooks a chronicle and evaluation of what they have read. They write personal reactions, questions, reflections, interpretations, connections with past experiences, predictions, summaries, and the like. These response journals then can serve as a reference source for assessment portfolios; as a source for future creative writing; as a way for students to see the process of how they get meaning from text and that they can take charge of their own learning. Instructors can assist those who may need initial guidance by giving them some cueing questions initially. For example, "As you think ahead to our next chapter on "X" what do you predict the main focus will be?" This reminds them of the importance of prediction. "What surprised you in our reading today and why?" "What seemed significant to you? Explain." "With whom do you identify in this story and what is it about that character that triggers your feeling of identification?" This kind of coaching at the onset will help students eventually carry on automatically without prompts.

It is helpful to hold periodic Response Journal Conferences which are collaborative in nature. Here students share responsibility for making it purposeful and productive, possibly starting with a summary review since the last conference, then moving on to the student's agenda, a concern, question, problem, reaction. Next, views are exchanged as if talking with a colleague. A sample follows. "Let's discuss this together. Were your predictions met or not? ... Why do you suppose that was so? ... I can see how that might have happened as I might have predicted "Y". Isn't it interesting that "Z" ... Do you realize that when I read this the first time I wanted to learn more about "A" and since the text didn't tell me I had to find some other material. Has this ever happened to you?" ... You are modelling for them so that after that they can also lead the conversation.

A real bonus for the instructor is that in reading and reacting in conferences to these response journals important insights can be obtained. Reading these journals is never repetitious or boring as some assignments can be.

Strategy 2: Portfolios for Assessment

An old idea recently resurrected is the use of portfolios for assessing students. This collection of student work may include teacher entry and exit assessment, interest inventories, audio and video tapes of the student, writing samples, illustrative work, response journal, list of books or other materials read, student self-assessment plus several items students select as their best work.

We are all weary of too much of the kind of repeated assessment that has been the norm in the United States and is now part of the National Curriculum in England. Portfolios can be a refreshing alternative or a significant adjunct for determining student progress. The use of portfolios becomes a strategy in that students take an active role in determining what should be included and where they stand in the learning process.

Strategy 3: KWL PLUS

To help students master expository text, Carr and Ogle (1986) developed KWL Plus which shows readers the importance of background knowledge. Step K stands for what I already know, Step W for what do I want to know, and Step L for what I have learned. The plus pulls it together. The instructor first brainstorms with the class as to what they already know about the topic to be read, recording their responses on the board. A discussion of where they learned their facts or how these facts might be proved can be beneficial here. Students then try to group items on the board into general categories, which helps them store new data to be read under these labels. Step W helps to determine purpose for reading by having students write specific questions they want answered. After reading, students write what they learned and decide whether their questions have been answered. If not, further reading on the topic may be in order. The plus feature has students moving on to forming conceptual maps and summarizing the material.

Strategy 4: FLIP

To determine the personal readability of a text Schumm and Mangrum (1991) designed FLIP, which looks at four factors: friendliness, language, interest and prior knowledge. The intention is to help students become independent, strategic readers by being able to self-evaluate how difficult their text is to them. "Friendliness" merely stands for how easy to comprehend; "Language' for how difficult the language is in terms of structure and vocabulary; "Interest" looks at their own motivation to read it; and "Prior knowledge" reminds them to think of how much they already know about the subject or specific topic.

Strategy 5: SAVOR (Subject Area Vocabulary Reinforcement)

Stieglitz and Stieglitz (1981) describe an interesting vocabulary strategy for clarifying terms, especially those which are frequently confused. To introduce this strategy, first take a familiar category of words, then elicit words from the students to fit the chosen category, having them list these in a column. Next, some features are written across the top to form a matrix. The squares are then filled in using a plus or minus sign to show connections. for example in Maths:

	curved lines	sides equal length	four sided
Square	–	+	+
Triangle	–	+	–
Rectangle	–	–	+
Circle	+	–	–

An advanced approach could use a numbering system (0 = none, 1 = a few, 2 = many, 3 = all).

Thus, looking back to our original acronym of "BUMS", we can attempt now to rate these randomly selected strategies as to which might be the most powerful or which might best meet specific needs of our students. Examine Table 1 to see if you agree or not. It would be interesting to continue this process with many other current, popular strategies!

Table 1. Strategy Rating

		Build Bridge	Use Knowledge of Text Structures	Monitor for Meaning	Summarize
1.	Response Journals	V	P	V	V
2.	Portfolios	V	P	V	V
3.	KWL PLUS	V	P	V	P
4.	FLIP	V	V	V	O
5.	SAVOR	V	O	V	V

Key: V - Very Evident
     P - Possible
     O - Not Likely

References

CARR, E. AND OGLE, D (1987) "KWL Plus" *Journal of Reading*, 30, 626-631.

EDWARDS, P.R. (1992) "Using Dialectical Journals to Teach Thinking Skills". *Journal of Reading*, 35, 312-316.

FYFE, R. AND MITCHELL, E. (1985) *Reading Strategies and their Assessment*, Windsor: NFER Nelson.

NEWTON, E.V. (1991) "Developing Metacognitive Awareness: The Response Journal in College Composition". *Journal of Reading*, 34, 476-478.

PEARSON, P.D. AND FIELDING, L.G. (1991) *Handbook of Reading Research.* New York: Longman, Vol.2, 815-860.

SCHUMM, J.S. AND MANGRUM, C. (1991) "Flip: A Framework for Content Area Reading." *Journal of Reading*, 35, 120-124.

STIEGLITZ, E.L. AND STIEGLITZ, V.S. (1981) 'Savor the Word to Reinforce Vocabulary in the Content Areas". *Journal of Reading*, 25, 46-51.

TONJES, M.J. (1991) *Secondary Reading, Writing and Learning.* Needham Heights, MA: Allyn and Bacon.

TONJES, M.J. AND ZINTZ, M.V. (1992). *Teaching Reading, Thinking, Study Skills in Content Classrooms.* Dubuque, IA: Wm.C.Brown, 3rd.ed.

A Pressing Need to Read.

John Aldridge

It is a very humbling experience to be invited to write for experts in what after all is my stock in trade: words and spaces. The printed word is dear to my heart, not only for itself and its value as a guardian of the democratic and cultural process, but also for more years than I care to remember it has paid my salary and afforded me a challenging and fulfilling career!

The regional press has, since the middle of the eighteenth century, been the basic core of community life and I am happy to be able to report to you that today its role is unaltered. Local radio, indeed local TV, has been around for some time but we still have local papers which have, in the case of *The Cornishman* in Penzance for example, a 97% household penetration: that is newspaper speak for 97% of households in that region buying the paper.

My colleague, the Managing Director of the *Carmarthen Journal* tells the wonderful story of how, on the day that Queen Victoria died, one lady in a tiny Welsh village failed to get her newspaper and then, though her neighbours told her that the Queen had died and that was why all the curtains in the village had been drawn, she would not believe it until she read it in the paper! This sort of feeling is still abroad: 39% of people surveyed recently said that the local and regional press gave them information that is most trustworthy. The next highest score was television with 16%.

During 1991/92 it was my privilege to be the President of the Newspaper Society, the trade organisation representing the local and regional press. The local and regional press has 1,205 titles with a total paid-for circulation of 43,100,000 per week published in the UK. When elected President, it is possible to choose a theme for the Presidency: I chose "In Print In Mind". It has been my over-riding concern to encourage young people and illiterate adults to read.

I have addressed nine newspaper industry conferences and countless other meetings on this topic. The reaction of my colleagues who have worked with me to develop Newspaper in Education and literacy schemes has been heartening. There are now over 220 Newspaper in Education schemes in operation in newspapers of all sizes and descriptions in the United Kingdom working in all sorts of ways with educational institutions.

I have been impressed in my year of office by the care with which teachers, and I hope a growing number of parents, are helping children to discover the magic of the written word. I believe the local and regional press has an obligation in this process. After all, if we do not help we are denying ourselves a market in the future. It seems to me that helping people to learn to read is a straightforward commercial objective which we as an industry ignore at our peril.

Current illiteracy figures of 5.5 million are frightening. Initially I felt that the numbers were so huge that nothing could be done for these people. I worked closely with ALBSU in my Presidential year, and every time we updated the figures and had a new slide made for another speech and yet another conference, I began to find that my initial fear was diminishing. We can, and I hope with your help will, do something to help them.

In order to better assess the needs and aspirations of young people, we have recently undertaken a major survey of 3,250 pupils to find out their reading habits. This again was an education/industry link, a joint venture between Northcliffe Newspapers and Cheltenham and Gloucester College of Higher Education.

We are indebted to the students and staff who worked on the project and without whom we could not have conducted the research. I must also thank Graham Woodham, the Managing Director of Parker Tanner Woodham, who gave a whole day of his time to brief the students. We have not finished the analysis yet but I offer you the following figures as examples of what young people do and feel:

Of the 12 to 13 year olds, 84.7% watch TV every day and 97% watch most days; whilst over 50% play video games every day or most days. It is interesting, though unsurprising however, that 'Neighbours' has more attraction than other programmes. 66.5% of these young people watch 'Newsround' between 5.00pm and 5.30pm but only 9.5% watch the 5.40pm 'ITN News'.

The research gives some hope for the printed word. Of the 603 11 to 13 year olds commenting on the statement, "I enjoy TV more than reading", 59% agreed or strongly agreed, but a reassuring 41% had doubts as to the truth of it for them.

"I only read when told to", had an even more categoric response, 71.5% of the sample disagreed with this statement, whilst 69% thought reading was interesting. A further 49.5% disagreed that reading was only something they did for school work and 66.8% said reading is FUN.

We shall use the results of these, and other surveys we are funding, to guide us commercially, but we feel that you might wish to use them as well.

As an industry we are attempting to produce newspapers which will be attractive to the young reader. Obviously many schools, driven by the National Curriculum requirements to encourage pupils to 'write for a purpose and to a given audience', wish to publish their own newspapers. We have been able to help - after all, we have the technology!

The *Langton Green Gazette*, published for Langton Green School by the *Kent and Sussex Courier*, has been chosen by the National Curriculum Council as an exemplar of good practice in delivering Technology at Key Stages 1 and 2. My colleague, Keith Harcourt, has edited the book, 'A Teacher's Guide to Making a Newspaper', to help teachers do this easily.

In Cheltenham, Exeter and Barnstaple, we publish regular supplements written and marketed by and for young people. Neither is this effort confined to the United Kingdom. Our colleagues at *Le Republic Lorrain* produce 'Le Cartable' and all around the world other papers are engaged in similar projects. The aim is still to help young people and adults to read.

While reading this I hope that you will be formulating ideas, because I believe that if we put our commercial resources and your educational expertise together we will have a formidable force with which to combat the problems we address.

As I prepared this contribution I thought I had better find out a little about the UKRA and one of the things my colleagues supplied me with was your book "Reading Together". I was particularly taken by the sentence in Derek Thackray's contribution, "Criteria for a reading scheme": "Children often indicate by their comments that reading is something they do outside of the reading scheme!"

My good friend and colleague, John East from Lancashire Weekly Newspapers, would certainly be able to substantiate that particular comment. Some research done in his Newspaper in Education project indicated very clearly that where parents do not buy a newspaper, but where the young people used a newspaper in school, the youngsters were spending their own pocket money to buy a newspaper. They clearly see the advantage and use it - and we are talking about eight to ten year olds.

The local newspaper certainly is not a graded text book but it is a real text. It is about people that children know and about things that happen where they are. We have mounting indications that children place a great deal of importance on reading real text.

But newspapers are not written for children, I hear you say, and again "Reading Together" helps me. John Mann's piece, "Hard Writing - Easy Reading", should perhaps become required reading for journalists. I was also delighted to see another piece which quotes from James McCulloch's "Meanwhile Gardens", because it illustrates a philosophy that we have employed in persuading our colleagues, teachers, and children to work with us to improve reading skills. McCulloch says, "People first, materials and equipment next, money last". He talks about getting people interested, tapping the sources of publishing materials and also the sources of what industries see as waste. Now I know that the piece is being used as an example of simple writing but the philosophy is the one which has enabled newspapers to go forward and work together with educationalists on the opportunities of reading. Notice I have changed the word; they are not problems, they are opportunities.

I accept, of course, that most newspapers are not written for children, though some parts of them may be. One newspaper writes an article each week to a reading age of eight and sets it in Sassoon Primary, an easy to read typeface, especially to make it easier for young people to gain something from the paper.

If you tell us that is what is required we will talk to our Editors and see if we can make it happen. But as John Mann says, "Writing like this is hard work", so it may be that we shall have to work hard to do it. Alongside all of this is the fundamental message of NIE that the newspaper is a real life, renewable and cheap resource, to be used in classrooms.

Debbie Biddle, a teacher employed for two years at the *Huddersfield Daily Examiner*, has written a book, 'Using Newspapers in the Classroom', which, whilst it has ideas directed at Key Stages 1 and 2, is applicable to all Key Stages and subjects by a simple process of extension.

Now let us look in one broad brush stroke at education. The average size of a teaching class in primary schools in 1989 was 25.7; by my crude mathematics, given that each class only has one teacher, that means that the individual attention gained by any one child in any one hour can only average out at 2.33 minutes. Now I know that teachers have many different strategies for making sure that children get as much individual attention as possible but it does seem to me that we have to look very carefully at any methods of teaching reading which make extra time. One such strategy is getting children reading outside the classroom. If we can persuade parents that the newspaper is readily accessible text with which they can attempt to help their children learn to read, then we will at least have taken one step on the journey.

There is good evidence in the United States and elsewhere, that the children of families where the parents have a history of learning difficulties are more likely to have learning difficulties themselves. We as an industry also have research that shows that what people with reading difficulties most often wish to read is the newspaper, so perhaps we might be able to help both.

In the book, 'Active Learning', which is in use in my industry, Jill Baldwin makes the point which is transferable into today's topic. She says, "I believe that the trainer starts out holding much of the responsibility for what is going to happen on a course. At the beginning they are responsible for any development, personal or professional, that is going to take place, but they need to be continuously looking for ways of encouraging the group to take on that responsibility for themselves." Now I believe that this is totally applicable to children and to their learning to read. The parents and the teacher do, at the beginning of a young life, have to hold much of the responsibility, but there is a crucial need to enable the children to take responsibility for their own learning. The best place for that to happen is outside the classroom, using materials applicable and relevant to the world that exists outside the classroom. Indeed Carl Rogers put it rather neatly when he said, "I know I cannot teach anyone anything, I can only provide an environment in which he or she can learn." Let's try and do that in thousands of homes!

I believe that together we could provide such an environment, working on what I can only call a 'something' which might allow us to address the opportunities for children and adults to access text in a totally new, exciting and diverting way. The medium already exists, the newspapers are there and we can use them. We may have to try to find ways of providing slightly different text but it must remain local, referring to the reader's own community, or it will lose its unique selling point.

I would like, therefore, to invite you to use our commercial expertise, to use our newspapers to open more doors for more people to learn to read. We have made a start on our own, with your co-operation we can go much further.

Readers wishing to know more about Newspapers in Education are invited to contact: Northcliffe NIE Project, Tower Lodge, Sandown Park, Tunbridge Wells Kent. TN2 3HZ Telephone: 0892 512321.

Encouraging Reading as a Lifelong Habit

Keith Nettle

At the end of the perennial British radio show, Desert Island Discs, castaways are offered a book and a luxury, in addition to the Bible and Shakespeare, which cannot be refused (even by atheistic philistines). It is a well tried formula, making comfortable assumptions about our cultural heritage, as mediated by Radio 4. How safe is the book element in this value system, or in the wider contexts we might want to propose?

In this paper I shall briefly examine the state of reading and the printed word in the UK, paying some attention to the supposed threats to the reading habit which are commonly advanced. For the British government, the perceived danger seems to be falling educational standards; to some observers, the threat is competition from other media and new technology; others see contemporary lifestyles, particularly those of the young, as alien to books and reading.

I shall range beyond education quite deliberately. In the first place this is because I am a publisher and not a professional educator, and secondly it is because I believe that, while education has a critical role to play, reading as a lifelong pursuit depends on many factors and influences outside education. I shall argue that literacy worldwide, and book appreciation in this country, will only flourish through an alliance of public and private interests, as proposed in an international Charter for the Reader which I shall introduce.

Bruno Bettelheim and Karen Zelan have defined the two basic uses of literacy as follows: "There are two ways in which reading (and the learning of it) can be experienced: either as something of great practical value, important if one wants to get ahead in life; or as the source of unlimited knowledge and the most moving aesthetic experience." (Bettelheim and Zelan, 1982)

Government's emphasis for some time has been upon 'practical value' in its crusade to improve reading standards. Deeply suspicious of the 'trendy' or 'liberal' teaching methods to whose excesses it attributes a supposed fall in standards, its disowning of the LINC project and latest insistence on changes to the English curriculum has worried many moderate commentators by the simplistic nature of its linguistic assumptions. The Secretary of State for Education warned against English being 'a voyage of self-discovery' for children. Yet no contradiction was apparently seen in this same person's instruction to the National Curriculum Council to include not only more phonics and grammar, but also 'good books' -

works surely concerned above all with 'self-discovery'!

I shall not attempt to go into the whole tangled question of reading assessment, despite some personal involvement on the publishing side. What we seem to be seeing is a staged retreat from the original Government-approved criterion-referenced model, as it has progressively been realised by those in power that criterion-referenced reading tests will not produce the sort of normative or comparative results which age-related standardised reading tests do. Perhaps it would better serve the cause of reading standards in the truest sense if the English curriculum could be unfettered in its coverage of language and literature, practicality and creativity, while the monitoring of performance and standards was annually checked by means of established standardized reading tests.

The methods debate over teaching reading shows no sign of abating, as correspondence in the UKRA Newsletter *Language and Literacy News* demonstrates. In the long term, it seems unlikely in itself to have a decisive effect on the survival or disappearance of the printed word. Most children appear to pick up their concepts about print from supermarkets or hamburger takeaways, and learn to read somehow - at any rate to the level needed for the tabloid press, technical literature relevant to their jobs and cars, or popular fiction. The minority who do not learn to read without individual attention clearly have special educational needs, and I suspect that the issue of the most effective teaching method only becomes critical in such cases (which isn't of course, to deny that good teaching is infinitely more vital and interesting for all children than mediocre teaching, or that children's enthusiasm for books can clearly be fostered by a rich book environment at school as well as at home).

Information technology is sometimes seen as a threat to much book-based reading. As improved computerised systems are developed for the storage, display and manipulation of text and illustrations, a question mark hangs over certain types of non-fiction publishing. However, wherever extensive reading is involved, the book retains enormous convenience and legibility, while the brilliant wordsearch, cross-referencing and split-screen devices increasingly available on computers still fail to facilitate the sort of natural thumbing backwards and forwards through the pages of a book which remains one of the greatest technical features of the medium.

A British Library research study provides evidence to counteract any dichotomy between book reading and handling text in computers which might seem to draw young people away from books. The researchers, Carolyn Carter and Jenny Monaco, investigated the use of various forms of information technology in primary and secondary schools. They found that the pupils who worked most successfully with IT were those who were also fluent readers, and that the good readers were those who read for pleasure, quite apart from their school work.

"Regardless of age, all those pupils who successfully skimmed and scanned resources for information (rather than having to read every word or erratically reading bits of text) were fluent readers of print on paper. Those observed in a library context appeared to be comfortable in such an environment and at ease with handling resources, especially books. Such pupils were also the ones who tended to utilise indexes and directories of their own accord, and their approach when searching for keywords appeared to be the same whether they were using a printed or an electronic resource. According to the staff and pupils, many of the children had not been formally taught to use such techniques but had discovered them whilst using books for their own purposes and had unthinkingly transferred them to school work." (Carter and Monaco, 1987)

The beauty of this finding is that it destroys any notion of opposition between books and computers, or between leisure reading and study reading. We can confidently assert that the reading habit should be encouraged not only for its intrinsic value to the individual but also for the practical benefits it produces in terms of information technology and many other contemporary needs.

Another factor seen as threatening the reading habit is competition from other entertainment media, particularly television. It has been claimed that regular viewing especially of commercial TV, with relatively short programme segments interrupted by groups of advertisements, leads to an impatience with, or even inability to adjust to, activities requiring a longer attention span. The research evidence on this, however, is far from clear-cut. According to a group of American researchers, 'Televiewing accounts for little variance in achievement: it is neither the 'villain' or the 'redeemer' some have claimed' (Williams, Haertel, Haertel & Walberg, 1982). As far as leisure reading is concerned, also, the '3-minute culture' case does not seem totally convincing. Long films are shown on television, often on the BBC without advertisement breaks; while many of the most popular authors dominating the bestseller lists write enormously long novels - 'blockbusters' - which people must presumably be reading in reasonably long stretches at a time.

Another concern which is often heard, but again has not been conclusively proved, is the theory that TV viewing is displacing reading among both children and adults. It must be the case that if many people of all ages watch television for several hours a day, as is known to happen, that must limit the time they have available for other activities. Research directly investigating this question, however, has found children's reading of books to be less affected than some other activities, such as listening to the radio, going out to see friends, or reading comics (Sharman, 1979).

Publishers and booksellers also have direct experience of the positive effect on book sales of TV tie-ins or TV-related books. The serialisation of a classic novel on TV invariable leads to increased sales of the book, and many other types of TV programme including documentaries, sport, cookery, and comedy, lead to book spin-offs the frequent success of which makes it clear that viewing and reading can be complementary pastimes.

I feel that in encouraging reading as a leisure habit we need to avoid the denigration of television (or any other legitimate entertainment medium), and yet should stress the unique experiential value of reading. Fiction on the page offers the reader the chance to form his or her own imaginative reconstruction of the author's work, which for many people can provide a deeper satisfaction than that derived from watching a dramatisation of the same work.

It is interesting to notice how many travellers buy a large novel to read on an intercontinental flight. For many years now, airlines have offered both feature films and multi-channel audio programmes on long flights, and yet many people still find satisfaction in immersing themselves, individually and privately, in a novel. A current Traveller's Handbook has this advice about a long flight: "The time will pass more quickly, and you'll feel better for it, if you get well into an unputdownable novel before leaving home and try to finish it during the flight." (Gorman, 1991)

This is surely something which should give us food for thought as we try to sustain and nurture the reading habit in other situations. We may need to emphasise not only the points of similarity between reading and competing forms of entertainment, although these certainly exist in terms of interest, excitement, and so on; but also the differences, of which the most significant is perhaps the 'privateness' of the reading experience - the possibility reading offers of withdrawal, for a time, from the public world we mostly inhabit, or even the family situation in which most people watch television, into what Bettelheim and Zelan (1982) call 'the new worlds opened to the mind and imagination through books'.

If we look for objective evidence of the national reading pattern, the overall value of books sold, and the health of publishing and bookselling businesses must be significant. According to the Publishers Association, using Business Monitor figures as well as returns from publishers, the total value of all UK publishers' sales in 1991 was £2.5 billion. This was a rise of about 5% on 1990 (which had shown a fall from the 1989 total). After allowing for inflation, the 1991 total represents a rise of about 14% over 1983.

In a period of recession, this hardly suggests any overall decline in book purchasing either currently or over the past decade. Publishing has been through a period of unparalleled takeovers and mergers, often painful for authors and staff alike, as most power has been concentrated in a few large groups such as Reed, Thomson, Pearson, Murdoch or Random House. For the reading public, however, there cannot be said to have been any serious reduction in the range or quality of books available, even if prices have risen at an above-average rate. On the contrary, the marketing resources of the large publishing houses has combined with the expansion of bookselling chains such as Dillons and Waterstones, to markedly improve the quality of bookshop siting and display in many modern shopping areas. A particularly encouraging development as far as children's reading is concerned is the decision of the major supermarket chains - Sainsbury's, Tesco and Safeway - to stock well produced children's books and sell them at low prices. This is a long way from the Desert Island Discs book choice, but it is even more culturally significant, making it as natural for parents and children to buy a book as any other product from the supermarket shelves.

It is of course possible to paint an over-optimistic picture of the reading and book-buying scene. There are still pockets of illiteracy in Britain, and continuing illiteracy on a massive scale in much of the developing world, where the challenge is to link literacy with maternal hygiene, and teach parents and children together. In the advanced countries, we are no nearer to any real understanding of what makes some people lifelong readers, while other, equally intelligent people hardly ever pick up a book. No convincing correlation has to my knowledge been traced between sensitivity to literature and sensitivity in personal relations, even though it could be argued that classic literature is above all concerned with the question of how to live. More worryingly, there is no sign that books play any role in reducing the sense of alienation from society felt by rioting youths on urban housing estates.

What we can assert is a correlation between effective reading of books and educational and career success. In the Bettelheim formulation, reading is 'of great practical value, important if one wants to get ahead in life'. What also seems likely is that extensive leisure reading benefits reading for practical purposes: the more a person reads, and the more pleasurable the activity, the more effectively he or she reads. In a recent APU report based on research in 1800 schools, a positive correlation was found between children's initial enjoyment of the books they read and later high scoring in reading and writing tests (APU, 1991). It is clear that advanced societies demand a high level of literacy from their professional and commercial workforces and that this is best achieved by encouraging reading for pleasure from the beginning.

In consideration of the issues I have been discussing, the International Publishers Association (IPA), to which the British P.A. (including the Educational Publishers Council) are affiliated, has set up a Reading Committee which meets twice a year to monitor developments in reading in the various countries represented, and to share ideas for the encouragement of reading. I serve as the PA's representative on this committee, whose main initiative so far has been the drawing up of a Charter for the Reader, which was adopted by the IPA Congress in New Delhi in January 1992, and is likely to be adopted and disseminated by UNESCO. (IPA, 1992).

The Charter opens by asserting the universality of the right to read, in the context of education and the need to combat global illiteracy. This basic right is justified by brief statements of the influence of reading culturally and scientifically, socially, democratically and in terms of individual creativity.

The second section is headed **Opportunities for Reading**. Clearly the universal right to read can only become a reality if certain conditions are fulfilled. The first condition is the need for pre-school children to encounter books, ideally with their parents at the earliest possible age. 'This is how reading books becomes an important, familiar and intimate experience, a way of communicating with those who are close, a way of understanding the world and oneself.' Part 2 of this section deals with **Access to books in schools**, emphasising the need for professionally run school libraries with books of wider interest, in addition to class libraries and subject text books. Youth education outside school is also mentioned.

The third section of the Charter covers **Support and Encouragement for Reading**. It outlines the type of support which is desirable from the various professionals and agencies who effect the situation. Governments head the list because, in the words of the Charter, they can help to provide 'an environment in which books can flourish' through fiscal measures, attitudes to school funding, libraries, copyright, and so on. Writers and translators are naturally included, both for their original creative contribution, and the role many play in the promotion of their own and other books, for example in 'writers in residence' schemes. Publishers and booksellers are of course commercially motivated, but it is essential to include their role in the overall scene, since their support for reading, which is a matter of self-interest, is also critical to the needs of readers. To take an obvious example, bookshops such as Waterstones brought a new atmosphere to British bookselling by staying open late and providing a comfortable setting and attractive displays. Their motive was to increase their sales, but the benefit to many book buyers was considerable. Libraries, from their different perspective, have also worked hard to provide an attractive environment for borrowers, and the Charter emphasises the value of libraries appealing to all age-groups and situations. In both bookshops and libraries the importance of trained and knowledgeable staff is highlighted. The Media are mentioned on account of their role as presenters of books to the public.

The fourth and final section of the Charter for the Reader is headed **Information**

and Co-Operation in Reading. It draws together the various threads of the document, emphasising the desirability of an alliance of public and private interests and a life-long perspective as regards the reading environment.

The Charter ends on what we hoped was an inspirational note, in the assertion that 'books are the spiritual powerhouse of humanity - the resource that can enable humanity to face the future with confidence. Books need - books deserve - universal interest and support.'

The International Publishers' Association's Charter for the Reader has the limitations of an internationally devised document which has to cover a variety of national situations. I believe that, nevertheless, it does manage to address the main players and influences in the reading arena, and to point to the obligations that need to be met and the conditions that need to be fulfilled, if the reading of books is to grow in the next century as it has during the previous five.

On our desert island, or rather in the Global Village which is now the cultural context of literacy, we must ensure that the book choice remains on offer.

References

A.P.U. (1991) *Language for Learning (Assessment Matters No.4).* London: H.M.S.O.

BETTELHEIM, B. and ZELAN, K. (1982) *On Learning to Read: the Child's Fascination with Meaning.* London: Thames and Hudson.

CARTER, C. and MONACO, J. (1987) *Learning Information Technology Skills* (Literacy and Information Research Report 54). London: The British Library.

GORMAN, S. (ed.) (1991) *The Traveller's Handbook.* London: Wexas.

International Publishers' Association (1992) *'Charter for the Reader' International Publishers Bulletin (Vol. VIII, No. 2).* Geneva: International Publishers' Association.

SHARMAN, K. (1979) *Children's Television Behaviour: its Antecedents and Relationship to School Performance.* Hawthorne, Victoria: Australian Council for Educational Research.

WILLIAMS, P., HAERTEL, E., HAERTEL, G. and WALBERG, H. (1982) 'The Impact of Leisure-Time Television on School Learning: A Research Synthesis' *American Educational Research Journal*, Vol. 19, No. 1.

The Teacher's Role in Early Literacy Learning

Ros Fisher

Whilst a great deal has been written in recent years about the literacy contexts of classrooms, the focus has tended to be on the reading material and the physical environment. Less has been written specifically about the teacher. In fact certain writers have tended to under play the role of the teacher in relation to the importance of interesting reading material. Liz Waterland's 'It is the book that will do the teaching' (1985, p16) implies less importance to the role of the teacher. Indeed, since Plowden (1967) with its emphasis on learning, there has been a certain fear of overemphasis on the role of the teacher. This, together with criticism from certain areas, particularly the press and right wing lobbyists, has left those teachers who place the child at the centre of their teaching and who adopt a whole language approach uncertain as to their role.

I have been interested to try to find out what makes a successful teacher of early literacy, having been myself a teacher, through the process of using a single reading scheme based on control of sight vocabulary, through context support schemes to colour coding a variety of scheme and 'real' books. It fascinates me to remember that children learned to read even though I was using a reading scheme that went against all my present knowledge of how children learn. I also like to think that children left my classroom with a genuine love of books and an interest in reading. Since I left classroom teaching the use of reading schemes has been called into question, those that are published now are certainly much more interesting than they used to be but I really do wonder whether I would use one if I were teaching now, given the range of excellent non-scheme books for children.

In my attempt to discover what it is that makes a successful teacher of early literacy I have considered research into the three aspects of the problem: the task, the child and the teacher. I have also considered the National Curriculum as this is bound to have an impact on what teachers do, certainly in British classrooms.

Firstly, the task: what do we actually mean by literacy?
This is important since our definition shapes our teaching. By reading do we mean word recognition or do we mean making meaning - and is this what we mean right from the time the child starts school? Most people will agree on the importance of deriving meaning from the text but many will not agree that this is important for young children starting to learn to read. All this also relates to our view of learning about literacy - are we concerned with a utilitarian view of literacy or a personal one? Is reading taught solely with the intention of enabling the child, once an adult, to use that reading for the purpose of survival and advancement in society. Or does

reading have a value for the individual over and above its utilitarian function? In fact most teachers' views will be somewhere along a continuum between the two poles described above.

Debates rage fiercely, now as always, about the best ways to enable children to learn to read. Government ministers make statements about what should happen in the classroom; although these seem to tell us more about their own experience of schooling than any understanding of how children learn. The press describe classrooms that do not sound like any I have ever seen. Educationalists may take sharply contradictory yet largely theoretical standpoints; and in the middle are the teachers trying to do their best for the children who pass through their care.

In my mind the debate about the task of literacy learning revolves around three issues: 'real books' versus reading schemes, the teaching of skills, and the acceptability of error.

The debate about 'real books' as opposed to reading schemes is surely a red herring. The important factor must be what materials, from a full range of reading matter, are provided and how they are used. I have seen flash cards and 'word tins' used with 'real books' and excellent teachers creating excitement and interests with 'One, Two, Three and Away'. The more recently published reading schemes attempt to provide interest for the reader, rely on context and provide a range of support materials such as big books and taped stories. Both reading schemes and so called 'real books' can be used well or badly according to the individual teacher. More important is the provision of a wide range of reading material and the messages given to the child about reading.

The teaching of skills is a subject that causes much discussion. However, despite the debate that surrounds this issue, decisions made by the teacher relate more to how the child will best learn to use the skills, not whether they should be learned. In theoretical terms there are two opposing schools which might be summarised as the behaviourist school and whole language exponents. In practice, teachers again fall somewhere along a continuum from one extreme to the other. Despite the differing standpoints, a general trend can certainly be observed in infant classrooms. There has been a shift from a belief that children needed to be taught certain skills and given decontextualised practice of those skills before they could use them, to the belief that children should be allowed to use, practice and learn skills at the same time. For example, whereas children used to have to learn to sight read certain words by practice on flash cards before they could be given a book to read, now they will be allowed to read and enjoy books at the same time as practising reading in context and being taught to recognise certain words through shared reading.

The tolerance of error is another issue that causes great concern about the lowering of standards. It is easy to understand how some parents who may have enjoyed reading one child's correctly spelled writing may be concerned when a second child brings home writing that has many unmarked spelling errors. Without an understanding of the beliefs and practice behind this, concern is understandable. Yet explanation and open discussion can explain how the second child is learning strategies for spelling and a sense of ownership of her writing whereas the first child may have had to rely on the teacher for spelling and judgement on her work. Fortunately the National Curriculum allows for and even requires examination of error behaviour. This is encouraging, for not only does a tolerance of error enable children to develop their own strategies, but the errors made in both reading and writing give invaluable information to the teacher about a child's learning.

Thus the teacher's conception of the task will affect how she teaches. Her confidence in her role will enable her to work effectively despite criticism and to explain to parents and interested observers why she is working as she is.

A second factor of obvious interest is the child who is central to the whole enterprise - though one could be forgiven for forgetting this in the light of media hype which centres on what teachers do (and do not do), what parents think and what society needs. In my musing about how literacy is learned I have considered what I took to be major influences on current views of teaching and learning:

(i) writers who have advanced our thinking about children's learning
(ii) research into the influence of home background

Taking first advances in our thinking about children's learning, following from Piaget, and particularly the more recent work of McGarrigle and Donaldson reported in Donaldson (1978) the child is viewed as an active learner endeavouring to make sense of her environment. Also influential is the work of Vygotsky which emphasises the role of speech as a foundation for thinking, the importance of shared social behaviour and the importance of co-operation with an adult to open up the zone of proximal development. Similarly Jerome Bruner's work emphasises the value of social interaction, the importance of the communicative intent, i.e. that the child desires to succeed in communication and the role of the parent to provide a framework (scaffolding) for learning - contexts and routines that are familiar to the child.

From this we gain a picture of a child who is actively concerned with making sense of her world and that talk underpins this. Also that learning is a shared activity and should not be undertaken in isolation. further it seems that the child will learn more in co-operation with an adult than might be thought possible from Piagetian stages of development.

The home background from which the child comes is also of importance when considering the best ways to enable her to learn. The work of Tizard and Hughes (1984) and of Gordon Wells and the Bristol Language Project (1984 amongst others) has dispelled the deficit theory which operated in the sixties and seventies and in which the child was viewed from the point of view of what was missing and needing remediation. We now acknowledge the value of all children's pre-school experience and recognise the importance of what the child brings to the task of literacy learning.

Studies of the difference between learning at home and at school show us that in the home the child initiates the learning through activity that is meaningful to her. In the home the learning takes place in contexts of sharing and reciprocity and is related to the child's previous experience. There is also appropriate feedback and encouragement given.

This has implications for teachers who need to take into account what the child brings to the task. She is already an active learner who is capable of and successful at learning. She lives in a print rich environment and has had experience of this in a whole range of contexts before starting school. She has had experience of storying through listening to family conversation and from television. these three are vital ingredients to literacy learning and cannot be ignored.

It is the teacher in whom I am most particularly interested. It is such a complex and beleaguered role. Teachers, whilst being aware of the theoretical and ideological stances, need to be making decisions in the classroom,hundreds of times a day, about what and how they enable the class, a group or a particular child to learn. In order to consider this role in more depth I have taken evidence from a variety of research studies and HMI reports produced in the 1980s as to what happens in classrooms. It should be noted that the research data reported is mostly associative and therefore does not necessarily provide causative evidence. This research does show, however, that the teacher can be an important predictor of achievement after home background factors are taken into account.

The following factors are ones that re-occur in these studies. There is not the space here to examine each in detail but a list can give pointers to the role of the teacher in early literacy. Further discussion can be found in Fisher (1992).

Factors found to be of importance in enabling effective learning
(findings from various research and published in the 1980's*)

• High level of interaction including opportunities for extended conversation and higher order questioning.
• Good match showing high expectations of ability and interest.
• Good task design and evaluation including consideration of cognitive outcomes.
• Good assessment and record keeping.
• Opportunities for co-operative learning.
• Feedback to children with praise and positive attitude.
• Whole school policies.
• Parental involvement.
• Management skills such as advance organisers, routine.
• Encouraging active involvement, allowing freedom to make errors and find solutions within a framework.
• Relevance and purpose to the task, discussed with and understood by children.
• Range of activities and approaches within literacy tasks.

(*Galton and Simon (1980), DES (1982 and 1989), Bennett et al (1984), Tizard and Hughes (1984), ILEA (1988), Mortimore (1988), Tizard et al (1988), Bennett and Kell (1989))

In addition to these factors teachers have to adhere to the National Curriculum programmes of study and attainment targets. While there is not space to consider these in detail here, a brief look at some of the underlying principles can show how these do follow from the developments in our understanding of children's literacy learning. Firstly, the range of literacy experience that children encounter is emphasised. Secondly, it is repeated that the context of children's literacy learning should be those of the child's own world. Thirdly, following the work of Bruner and Vygotsky, the importance of discussion is emphasised. Fourthly, it is stressed that the children's autonomy as learners should be developed.

The four elements that have been briefly considered here; those of task, learner, teacher and National Curriculum, point towards a definite and important role for the teacher. A role that does not necessarily adhere to one ideology or doctrine but one that is multi-faceted, responding to children as individuals, learning from but not being dictated to by educational theory, and making the best use of all the resources available.

This leads me to identify four principle roles for the teacher; those of facilitator, model, manager and assessor.

The teacher as facilitator will be concerned as to how the classroom is set up, what opportunities are available for children to use and experience literacy. She will influence the type of literacy tasks undertaken. Her view of language and how this is best learned will affect the children's learning. How the teacher responds to the child will also affect how that child views literacy and her role in it.

The teacher as model will provide an exemplar of the way literacy is used and enjoyed. She will demonstrate the skills of literacy by her own use in reading and writing in front of and alongside children. She will also demonstrate the wider role of literacy use by showing its use in the world outside the classroom and by her enjoyment of this.

The teacher as classroom manager needs to organise her classroom to take into account how children learn, both from her knowledge of theory and from her own experience as a teacher. She organises her classroom to allow individual interaction and cooperation, the active involvement of the children, use of resources, and opportunities for play. Her task design is also of importance in the learning that accrues from it and the message that it gives to the child about literacy.

The teacher as assessor does, and has always done, far more even that the onerous demands of the National Curriculum assessment procedures. Ongoing assessment is undertaken by the teacher both daily in an informal way and regularly in a more formal way, particularly by use of the observation of error behaviour. This assessment will require the active involvement of the child and the parents at points during the school year. It will also involve daily observation of the child's literacy behaviour in a variety of contexts. Also important is the feedback given to children, enthusiastic but genuine, appropriate and justified.

These roles are not isolated or employed in a serial way. Rather the roles are interrelated and the process cyclic. Thus, whereas the first decisions made by the teacher may be in the role of facilitator in relation to the environment of the classroom and the resources provided, this role will be supported by the role of manager and model which will be employed alongside the other roles on a daily basis. The role of assessor will be enabled by the other roles; it starts from the first encounter of child and teacher and continues throughout the school year. The observations and judgements made are then fed back into the other roles and affect the decisions made by the teacher as facilitator, model and manager.

Thus there is a role for the teacher. Not the highly didactic one demanded by the press and some other critics of current practice that sits uncomfortably with the tradition and experience of early childhood education. Rather a role that acknowledges the importance of the child and the way she learns, and that recognises the importance of the new understandings that we have developed about learning and literacy. Critics of the 'real books' approach are wrong to describe it as the 'minimalist teaching movement' (Donaldson 1989), when in reality it requires a great deal of hard work on the part of the teacher. Equally those are wrong who advocate a strict adherence to schemes which follow the agenda of a distant publisher rather than the child and the context. Teachers should have confidence from their knowledge of children and of relevant theory to provide the best possible opportunities for children to learn. They should have the confidence to provide a stimulating learning environment full of a wide range of literature. They should show children the skills and pleasure of literacy. They should develop the ability to manage the experiences that children have to enable them to learn to read and write skilfully and with pleasure. And they should learn to assess children's learning so that the other facets of their role can be carried out effectively. Many do this already and others will follow. There is nothing minimalist about this, nor is there anything overly didactic - merely a good teacher using her experience and knowledge to work hard to enable young children to move along the road to literacy.

References

BENNETT, N., DESFORGES, C., COCKBURN, A. AND WILKINSON, A. (1984) *The Quality of Pupil Learning Experiences*, London, Lawrence Erlbaum Associates.

BENNETT, N. AND KELL, J. (1989) *A Good Start? Four-year olds in Infant Schools.* Oxford, Basil Blackwell.

DES (Primary Advisory Council for Education) (1967) *Children and their Primary Schools* (The Plowden Report). London. HMSO

DES (1982) *Education 5 to 9: an illustrative survey of 80 First Schools in England.* London. HMSO

DES (1989) *Reading Policy and Practice at Ages 5-14: A Report by HM Inspectorate.* London, HMSO

DONALDSON, M. (1978) *Children's Minds.* London. London. Fontana.

DONALDSON, M. (1989) *Sense and Sensibility - some thoughts on the teaching of literacy.* Occasional Paper No.3. Reading and Language Information Centre, University of Reading.

FISHER, R. (1992) *Early Literacy and the Teacher*. London. Hodder & Stoughton.

GALTON, M. AND SIMON, B. (1980) *Progress and Performance in the Primary Classroom*. London, Routledge and Kegan Paul.

ILEA (1988) *The Hackney Literacy Study*. London, ILEA Research and Statistics Branch.

MORTIMORE, P., SAMMONS, P., STOLL, L., LEWIS, D. AND ECOB, R. (1988) *School Matters - The Junior Years*. London, Open Books.

TIZARD, B. AND HUGHES, M. (1984) *Young Children Learning: Talking and Thinking at Home and School*. London. Fontana.

TIZARD, B., BLATCHFORD, P., BURKE, J., FARQUHAR, C. AND PLEWIS, I. (1988) *Young Children at School in the Inner City*. London. Lawrence Erlbaum Associates.

WATERLAND, L. (1985) *Read with Me. An Apprenticeship Approach to Reading*. Stroud. Thimble Press.

WELLS, C.G. (1984) *Language Development in the Pre-School Years*. Cambridge, Cambridge University Press.

Story Writing and Young Second Language Learners: The Influence of Context and Control

Rebecca L. Huss

As teachers of young children, we have an important responsibility to provide our children with the best possible literacy learning environment that enhances and extends their language and literacy potential. An enhanced language and literacy learning environment is especially important for the increasing numbers of second language (ESL) learners in our classes who have to develop beginning literacy knowledge at the same time as they are acquiring a second language.

Despite the importance of teachers having a better understanding of the factors influencing ESL early literacy learning, very few studies have been done which have closely examined the beginning literacy learning of young ESL children within the classroom setting. Most of the classroom studies of early literacy have been done with native English speakers (Blazer, 1986; Dyson, 1989; Rowe, 1989); children in Spanish-English bilingual or ESL classrooms (Ventriglia, 1982; Hudleson, 1984), or with Southeast Asian refugees (Urzua, 1986; 1989) in the United States. While informative, these studies were done within very different educational environments and with different language groups than those faced by teachers within the United Kingdom. Very few published studies have been done in Great Britain with young Asian students and their acquisition of ESL literacy, especially in the area of beginning writing, yet these are the children that many U.K. teachers most frequently serve.

This paper which addresses some of the issues concerning beginning ESL writing is based on a portion of the results of a year long ethnographic study of the beginning literacy learning of five and six year old Punjabi speaking Pakistani students in a multi-ethnic primary school classroom in the north of England. The study's main focus was on children's beginning writing development, but explored various factors influencing the children's literacy learning both within and outside the school environment. As a participant observer, I sat around the writing table with the children, tape recorded their dialogue and regularly collected samples of their writing during various writing contexts. I also observed closely the teacher interaction with the children during various literacy interactions. The teacher in this class was a trained middle grades art teacher who was teaching out of field and therefore had limited background training and knowledge in beginning literacy, early childhood education or ESL.

As I later analyzed the data, two themes repeatedly emerged which proved to have a strong influence on the type of responses the children made to the writing they did in the classroom, context and control. These two factors were also found to ultimately influence what these young ESL learners could come to know about literacy learning in English.

The Importance of Context and Control

What are context and control and why are they so important, especially for second language learners?

Control concerns the decision making related to children's writing. Who is making the major decisions about their writing such as what children are to write about, and how they are to write it i.e. copy writing, teacher scribe writing, invented spelling? How much control do the children have to choose the topic and method, or does the teacher always make the major decisions?

Context concerns the types of writing children do and the reasons they do writing, i.e. writing story books, personal narrative writing, topic work expository writing, birthday and holiday cards, thank you notes among others. Key questions concerning context are: Do the children have the opportunity to experience many different types of writing? Do children mainly do the same type(s) of writing over and over again?

In considering the importance of these factors for beginning literacy learning of young ESL learners, it is first necessary to consider our beliefs about ESL children's beginning literacy learning capabilities. Often as educators who teach ESL children, it is very easy to underestimate their abilities and what they are capable of doing regarding English literacy learning. We tend to focus on all the things they cannot do, on what they do not know, in short, on their deficiencies. We form our notions of their deficiencies based on our perception of the amount of English they know; their home and family life, including their mother's English language and literacy knowledge i.e. "There is nothing going on in their home related to literacy, little that relates to school. Home is one place school is another place"; our perception of the importance we place on English language fluency for competence in literacy learning, i.e. "English first".

These perceptions, based on a cultural and linguistic deficiency framework, portray the prevailing message that because of these deficiencies, children are not capable of having much input or control over their writing, hence, we as teachers have to provide the control and limit the writing contexts. This perspective can lead us to provide our ESL children with a very limited teacher controlled literacy curriculum with very little opportunity for any child input or control over what they write or how they write it. For example, if we as teachers are not careful we can select the topics each time for children to write about, we also can lock children into a stage of copy writing (i.e. copying under the teacher's writing) and they have to wait for us to determine they are ready to move to the next stage.

Our selection of topics can easily fall into a narrow, repetitive pattern, such as each Monday having children write in their Monday News books what they did over the weekend, or having very limited assignments for topic writing. Consequently, children rarely, if ever are just given the opportunity to play around with print, or to write about anything they want to or to write using any method they want to. This was the case in my research classroom.

As I came to discover, by providing a very teacher controlled writing environment with limited contexts for writing, instead of enhancing their literacy learning opportunities in, we are really limiting our ESL children. They are limited in several ways:

Limited opportunities to learn about literacy. First, each new context or type of writing provides new opportunities for children to learn about how to express meaning in print. For example, how children responded to story book writing was very different from the responses to writing they gave when they wrote about what they did over the weekend.

Children learn about literacy by having opportunities to experiment with print, to form and test hypotheses about how print works, to interact with others during literacy encounters (Piaget, 1969; Vygotsky, 1962; 1978). When children are always given a teacher handwritten model of their story in the case of copy writing, or always given the specific topic to write about, the focus shifts from expressing meaning in print, to meeting the teacher's expectations to reproduce the handwritten model correctly or to write about the given topic in an acceptable way. Children are less likely to take risks, to experiment, to try new things such as invented spelling, to create new meanings as would be the case if they were given more control over their writing. This limited control thus limits the new literacy knowledge that they can acquire.

Limited access to literacy learning. Another potential problem of a highly teacher controlled writing program is that it can limit access to literacy learning for those children who are deemed, "not ready". It is very easy to underestimate what ESL children really know about literacy. Often, they know a lot more about literacy than for which we give them credit. If we as teachers are always the ones to make the decisions about what children are or are not ready for, and consequently withhold certain literacy experiences from them until they are ready, we often can deny children the opportunity to experience new literacy learning and to grow in their literacy understanding.

Since their opportunity for new literacy learning is limited, the view of the children as "not ready" is perpetuated. The results of lack of access to literacy was demonstrated by the case of "Iflaq". Iflaq was a summer birthday child, who at the end of the school year, had only been in the class three terms, as opposed to many of his peers' four or five terms. Initially, Iflaq had only beginning level English language and literacy skills. Because he was always considered "not ready" by the teachers, he was denied access to small group alphabet and phonics instruction, among various other literacy experiences during the course of the year. He was nevertheless expected to go up to the next grade level with the rest of the class having had much less access to literacy learning than many of the other "ready" children in the class. The same situation held for other young children in the class. Iflaq however, continued to be a motivated literacy learner and to progress in his literacy knowledge. He carried around a slip of paper with his name neatly printed on it that he had brought from home, so he could remember how to write his name. Despite the fact he requested to be able to move to the next stage in copy writing, he was required to remain at his present level two more months because he was deemed not "ready". Because of the teacher controlled writing contexts, the progress he did make despite the odds was discounted because it did not fit into the teacher's conceptual readiness framework.

Limited opportunities to demonstrate what they know. If children are always having to write about the same topics over and over without having any opportunity to write about what they want to write about, i.e. every Monday during Monday News the children must write about what they did over the weekend, or the always have to write on a teacher assigned topic, children are therefore only able to demonstrate what they know within the limited framework of the assignment. If the same writing contexts are repeated frequently, the teacher can easily come to think that the children's usual responses constitute the extent of their literacy knowledge, since they have to write the same types of things over and over. The cultural and linguistic deficiency stereotypes can be perpetuated and the children's actual literacy abilities and knowledge can be underestimated. In reality, children might know much more about literacy than they have been able to demonstrate, but have not been given a vehicle to express it. This point was vividly driven home by "Saira". Saira was one of the more advanced literacy learners in the class as demonstrated by her reading ability and by her ability to write many words on her own during writing using correct spacing, sentence structure. Despite having the mechanics of writing down, the content of her writing was the bare minimum. It usually consisted of a stylistic picture and one rather bland sentence such as "I played chasing with Asia". This was especially true of her Monday News writing.

In her interview about literacy, Saira confided in me that she hated Monday News because she was never taken anywhere and her family did not do anything over the weekend. She did not know what to write about. Monday News was very limiting for her.

When she was given the opportunity to write about anything she wanted to and in any way she wanted to for me on Thursdays as part of my research, a quite different picture emerged of Saira's writing. During the writing sessions she began to expand her writing topics to include her school friends and school events which she was not able to do before. She expanded her writing method to include phonemic invented spelling (writing on her own and spelling the words the way she thinks they sound). She had more varied peer interaction. Saira also began to take more risks in her writing to include stories that "weren't true". Previously, she had only written factual personal narratives. During Thursday writing, other children expanded their writing repertoires as well.

A more dramatic type of change took place at the end of the school year when the children were given an unexpected opportunity to write a teacher-scribed picture story book after seeing one in assembly written by a boy in another class. The children were eager to try one themselves so they were simply given three sheets of paper folded in half in the form of a book. They were free to write any type of story they wanted to.

The change in Saira's writing was dramatic. Gone were the stilted one line sentences of her previous personal narratives and in their place was rich dialogue and story language which formed the plot of her fantasy story, "Goldilocks the Baby", a take off of the original fairy tale. I was utterly amazed that Saira was able to tell a story like that.

What made the difference? First, it was a change of writing context. Saira and the other children were writing "books", not "stories" which, to them, connotated personal narratives. Books were different. They had a plot, a sequence, a special type of language. None of this was discussed before writing. The children were simply given the blank books and they created their own drawings and stories. They drew on their own "story schema" (Jensen, 1985) or knowledge of how stories worked which had been developing with their many experiences with books and stories both in and out of class.

Another factor at play here was that the children did not have to physically write the words themselves. I was there to write them for them as they told me the story. Their oral story telling freed them up from having to concentrate on both the mechanics of writing and the plot at the same time, which for young children is a substantial bonus.

Third, Saira and the children had control over their topics. They could write about anything they wanted to. They were not restricted to writing books on a given topic, hence, their imagination had free reign.

Implications for ESL Children's Writing

What does all this tell us about writing with young ESL children? First, it points to the importance that providing children a variety of writing contexts has on ESL children's writing responses. With each type of writing, children are able to draw on their past literacy knowledge and experiences. Saira's story book writing allowed her to tap into her story schema and knowledge of story language. The result was a very different type of response than she had previously given.

Control also plays a major role. When children are given control over their writing, what they write about and the method by which they write, children can then call upon and demonstrate the full extent of their literacy knowledge and experience. They begin to take risks and to make new literacy discoveries which further expand their English literacy repertoire. Children often demonstrate to us that they have more literacy knowledge than we had given them credit for. Previously, when the children in the class wrote using teacher controlled writing with limited topics and contexts, much of their literacy knowledge found no vehicle for expression and hence, remained hidden from view.

By focusing on child controlled writing and by featuring teacher scribe writing, it is not meant to imply that teachers should never assign writing topics to children or that teacher scribe writing is the preferred approach. There are times that it is appropriate for all children to write about a given subject, such as during topic work; just as it is necessary to provide a variety of methods by which children can write. The problem lies in always giving children the topic and method and giving them little control in the matter. Then, rather than helping our ESL learners, we are restricting them.

We need to offer our ESL children the broadest possible vehicles by which to express and to expand their literacy knowledge and experiences. When we focus on what ESL children do know and can do, and when we let them show us what they know with expanded contexts and more child control over their literacy learning, the results just might surprise us!

References

BLAZER. B. (1986). I want to talk to you about writing: Five year year olds speak. In B. Schiefflin & P. Gilmore (Eds.). *The acquisition of literacy: Ethnographic perspectives, Vol. XXI: Advances in discourse processes* (pp. 75-109). Norwood, NJ: Ablex Publishing Company.

DYSON, A.H. (1989). *Multiple worlds of childhood writers: Friends learning to write.* NY:Teacher's College Press.

HUDELSON, S. (1984). Kan yu ret an rayt en ingles: Children becoming literate in English as a second language. *TESOL Quarterly,* 18(2), 221-238.

JANSEN, M. (1985). Story awareness: A critical skill for early reading. *Young Children.* 41(1), 20-24.

PIAGET, J. & INHELDER, B. (1969). *The psychology of the child.* NY: Basic Books.

ROWE, D. W. (1989). Author/Audience interaction in the pre-school: The role of social interaction in literacy learning. *Journal of Reading Behaviour,* 21(4), 311-349.

URZUA, C. (1986). A children's story. In P. Rigg & D.S. Enright (Eds.). *Children and ESL: Integrating perspectives* (pp. 93-112). Washington, DC:TESOL.

URZUA, C. (1989). I grow for a living. In P. Rigg and V. Allen (Eds.). *When they all don't speak English: Integrating the ESL student into the regular classroom* (pp. 15-38). Urbana, IL: NCTE.

VENTRIGLIA, L. (1982). *Conversations with Miguel and Maria: How children learn a second language.* Reading, MA: Addison Wesley.

VYGOTSKY, L. (1962). *Thought and language.* Cambridge, MA: MIT Press.

VYGOTSKY, L. (1978). *Mind in Society: The development of higher thought processes.* Cambridge, MA: Harvard University Press.

Developing Children's Writing in a Context

Loreta Stewart

Over the past decade great emphasis has been placed on teaching writing as a process - from stimulus to final draft and publication. One process that is commonly taught involves six stages: brainstorm, plan, write, confer, redraft, publish. Pupils should be encouraged to try out this process, but they should also be given scope to test alternative approaches.

A research project carried out in Scottish schools has demonstrated the beneficial effect on the motivation and communicative competence of young writers brought about by couching their writing in a structured, yet flexible, context.

The experience gained from this study enables us to suggest how such an approach can best become a regular component of the writing programme in mainstream classrooms. Prerequisites and limitations are discussed as well as practical, organisational factors for the classroom teacher, with emphasis on its potential educational value.

Background to the study

It has long been recognised that learning to write (like any other learning) is facilitated if it takes place within a meaningful, stimulating context (Graves, 1983; Smith, 1982; Wells, 1983). The value of an effective context lies in the opportunities it affords:
(a) for teachers and children to cooperate in its creation, and
(b) for children to take on a degree of responsibility for their own learning - what they will learn, how they will learn, and at a pace to accommodate individual needs, interests and competences.

In creating a context, the roles of the teacher and the students are carefully defined: either party may initiate the theme/topic, although in practice this usually comes from the teacher, and may even be part of an overall plan devised by the school. The teacher orchestrates the development of the writing context by making time available to the students, by acting as guide, mentor, master-craftsman and provider of relevant resources. The children follow more-or-less parallel courses of study, each following the particular aspect of the theme he/she finds most interesting.

The range of activities afforded by the context are designed to ensure that common skills are practised. It could be argued that the work would be more powerful if children had total control and choice of subject matter, but this study is about writing in a context created between the teacher and the pupils. In the case of this study, the skills relate to writing in a variety of genres.

Certain assumptions have been made regarding the choice of stimulus or starting point for children's writing. The context referred to hereafter is based on an adventure simulation package - Wagon's West (Tressell Publications 1986). In general any commercially produced package would be a suitable stimulus for children's writing, provided the following criteria are met:
(i) there is a strong storyline which encourages active involvement: children working in pairs or small groups can engage in brainstorming as a pre-requisite to writing.
(ii) there are frequent opportunities for meaningful writing tasks with a clearly defined purpose and audience, albeit the children are mainly writing in role.
(iii) the storyline has sufficiently strong characters with which the children can readily identify: they can speculate, hypothesise and predict about the life style, experiences and relationships of people who lived in a place and time other than their own.
(iv) the topic encourages children to draw upon their imagination and prior knowledge, from fiction, television etc., to enrich the content of their own writing.

The study: Phase 1

The study was carried out in two phases over a period of two and a half years.

Phase I took place in 1990 and involved one secondary school in Scotland and its 4 associated (feeder) primary schools, approximately 120 pupils, 6 teachers and 2 researchers. The pupils were from P7 classes in the 4 primary schools: their class teachers agreed to take part in this pilot study along with two members of the English Department of the Secondary School.

It was the intention of the researchers to investigate the feasibility of using an adventure simulation package as a 'bridging unit' between Primary and Secondary language teaching. It was assumed that by using the same stimulus materials, and by making sure that P7 classteachers received the same in-service training relating to writing in a context, it would be likely to ease the transition of pupils from P7 to S1 and allow the S1 English teachers to assume a common baseline for further writing development. Since the focus was on the redrafting of children's writing and the use of a common 'correction code', joint planning sessions took place between the primary and secondary teachers.

Teachers were given a list of common writing activities (copy available on request) and guidelines towards a common correction procedure and teacher response.

The activities were carried out over one term, with fortnightly visits to separate primary schools by researchers and secondary English teachers. No 'tests' were administered before the pilot study began, but teachers were asked to keep dated samples of children's written work for later comparison.

The results of phase 1 of the pilot study were disappointing in so far as there was little evidence to support the original hypothesis. Despite the cross visiting by researchers/observers and the apparently common input from the 4 primary teachers the children's writing took off in all different directions. The idea of using a commercially produced package as a bridging unit was abandoned. With hindsight, I think this would happen with any group, primary, secondary or other.

However the class teachers involved in the pilot study reported positively on aspects of the children's writing behaviour which had been observed incidentally. All 4 primary teachers noticed a marked increase in the quality and quantity of pieces of writing from the majority of children in their class. This was borne out by comparison of dated work samples in individual children's writing folders. The teachers and the researchers/observers spoke of the enthusiasm for writing sessions that had developed in all 4 primary classrooms, and they also commented on the increased self-confidence of the children. We discussed the fact that the apparent increase in self-concept could be due to maturation and familiarity with the visiting teachers. It was also evident from classroom wall displays and from the children's behaviour in general that their enthusiasm for the writing project had spilled over into other curriculum areas, e.g. Art and Craft, History, Geography, Mathematics, Health Education etc.

In order to verify some of the relatively unsupported findings of the pilot study, a second study was set up.

Phase 2

This took place between January and Easter of 1992 and involved two primary schools in the Strathclyde Region of Scotland. Each school was monitored independently since they were located some distance apart and there was no opportunity for the teachers involved to meet. In school A there were two P6 classes of 30/31 pupils and in school B there was only one P6 class of 26 pupils. School A is situated in an area of multiple deprivation whereas school B draws its pupils from 'middle class' homes.

The three class teachers involved were given the same adventure simulation package, the same resources and the same instructions as in the pilot study.

Teachers were interviewed before the study began as to their expectations of the children's writing ability and their general behaviour while engaged in the writing task. They were also asked to keep a diary of the frequency of writing sessions and the pupils' comments and attitude as the frequency increased.

A random sample of pupils were interviewed as to their attitude to writing before the study began and when the study was drawing to a close. In the phase 2 study pupils were given the responsibility of compiling a 'folio' of dated pieces of work for comparison. Initially they sought confirmation from the teacher - "will this do for my folio?" - but latterly they decided independently which pieces should be included. This was taken as a sign of growth in self-confidence.

During this study the researcher visited the three classrooms on a weekly basis and sat in on the writing sessions: the classteacher and the researcher compared notes and discussed children's comments from time to time. These notes and examples of the children's work are the only documentary data available, but very often in action research anecdotal evidence and samples of work are the only evidence that can be obtained without disrupting the ongoing work of the class.

Findings

Perhaps the best way to present the findings is to compare a sample of teachers' comments before and after the study.

Table 1: Teachers' comments on pupils' willingness to write

Pre-Study	Post-Study
The children used to groan when I said 'take out your writing jotters'.	Children come and ask if they can write something for their project/folio.
It doesn't matter what you ask them to write about, the children always ask 'how long is it to be?'*	Nobody has asked 'how long has it to be?' for a long time.
Some children will do anything except write, and you're lucky to get 2 lines from them.	When they're not writing they're drawing or colouring in or talking about their writer folder.

*When children ask this question it usually means that the writing task is a chore that must be attempted to 'keep the teacher happy' i.e. quantity is more important than quality of learning.

Table 2: Teachers' comments on children's motivation

Pre-Study	Post-Study
I'll try anything that makes them enthusiastic about writing.	They've really enjoyed this project, and even the poorer group are proud of their writing folders.
I try to find something I think will interest the children but it doesn't always work out.	I've never seen them so animated - they live in the world of 'Wagons West' and they mention it throughout the day, every day, even when doing maths or PE.
James usually gives you one or two pages of very neat, but very boring, writing no matter what he's asked to write about.	James rushes through his work programme to get back to his writing folder. His last piece of work was 7 pages (A4) long and really exciting reading. His last diary entry (an integral part of the package) nearly made me cry.**

** Teachers were not asked to focus on individual learners but they invariably reported on those who showed a marked improvement in their enthusiasm and communicative competence.

The children's comments pre-study and post-study also endorse in the main what the teachers seem to be reporting -
• a significant increase in the children's willingness to write.
• the enthusiasm generated by their writing context pervades the whole school day. (Some children must also be talking about their work at home in the evenings because they bring in pictures for their topic drawn by big brothers and even fathers. This home involvement would have been understandable in the 'middle class' school, but teachers in the socially deprived area said this was the first time parents had shown any interest in what their children did at school.)
• children in all 3 classes appeared to develop a very positive self-image: teachers of this stage in the Primary say this is common at P6/7 but it was perhaps more noticeable because they were observing the children more closely because of the study.
• the responsibility for the compilation of an individual portfolio, and the fact that each child was allowed to decide which pieces to rework seemed to heighten their sense of ownership of their writing.

The teachers involved became increasingly motivated as the study proceeded. Initially they were asked to include a writing 'slot' in their timetable 3 times a week. By the fifth week of the study the writing sessions had become a daily feature of their programme; one teacher said the children insisted on writing sessions twice a day.

Implications for the classroom

"A psychodynamic approach to writing development rests on the understanding that, just as small children develop speech in a social environment in which they hear spoken language, attempt to use it themselves, receive responses to their efforts and recognise unconsciously how language can function for them, *so too writing development is best promoted within a similarly engaging and dynamic environment.*" (Arnold 1991)

In developing children's writing in a context, the choice of stimulus is extremely important. It must be appropriate to the particular group of learners, of real concern to them, and presented effectively. The criteria for the choice of a commercially produced package on which to base a dynamic context have already been discussed at the beginning of this article: problem solving situations arising from the context make an excellent springboard for brainstorming leading to purposeful writing. Ideally pupils move in and out of writing sessions throughout the day, as the rest of their work programme permits.

Pre-writing sessions should be informal, and pairs and groups form and reform as the task demands. Pupils may decide to move into a writing (or writing related) activity sitting in their seats, turning to their neighbours or creating social groups of three or four. Alternatively the teacher may wish to set aside a particular area of the classroom as a 'writing corner': pupils would decide whether or not they require to work there.

The teacher has the responsibility of planning for the smooth-running of writing sessions by providing and organising paper, pens, pencils, crayons etc. clearly labelled and accessible to promote independent learning. Pupils are responsible for the retrieval and return of the resources and their own writing folios. Some teachers suggested the addition of a check list attached to the outside of each child's folder as a simple record of the written pieces included: the teacher and the pupils could tell at a glance if the required 'genres' had been addressed.

The teacher moves about the class, helping out where necessary but keeping a low profile and **not** correcting mistakes in the surface features of children's work. (Attention to selected errors in spelling, grammar and punctuation may be best addressed at an individual pupil conference.)

The crucial role of self concept in any learning situation is now fully recognised. Teachers who know their classes well, instinctively know how to build their self confidence. They must also explore new audiences and means of publication and/or display of children's work to foster and maintain children's self esteem. Pupil expectations have to be deal with: learners who are used to very formal methods must be helped to come to terms with the 'new' classroom culture. Teachers, too, have to be more acutely aware of the inhibiting effect of constant on-going teacher correction.

The teacher's own belief in the value of writing is crucial: teachers may or may not see any value in writing stories, poetry etc. at their own level. Writing **with** the children should become an integral part of the teacher's language programme. We must never forget that we are the role models for the children we teach.

The kind of 'writing lessons' described in this study may differ from conventional practice in many Scottish classrooms. This is indeed a learner-centred approach. The pupil and the teacher cooperate, on equal terms, to create a dynamic context for writing. Writing in this way is beneficial to the individuals' ability for self-expression and contributes to personal growth.

Finally, this approach to children's writing helps them to use language in a real-life situation (albeit a simulation) and learning becomes much more than the acquisition of knowledge: by arousing a concern for values it helps to put the teaching of creative writing on the educational map.

References

ARNOLD, R. (1991) *Writing Development: Magic in the Brain* Milton Keynes: Open University Press.

GRAVES, D. (1983) *Writing: Children and Teachers at Work* Portsmouth, New Hampshire: Heinemann

SMITH, F. (1982) *Writing and the Writer* London: Heinemann

WELLS, G. (1981) *Learning Through Interaction: The study of language development.* Cambridge: Cambridge University Press

A critical look at classroom contexts for writing

Jane Medwell

The importance of context

In recent years much of the attention given to writing in classrooms has focused upon the provision of appropriate contexts. The National Writing Project concentrated upon classroom situations and gave a great deal of emphasis to the development of print-rich environments. The project has also encouraged a real interest among teachers in processes of writing and the use of authenticity in young children's classroom experience. Particular attention has been focused upon provision of authentic audiences and purposes for writing. The National Curriculum has been written in the context of much valuable work about writing and demands that children acquire a range of writing skills. The Curriculum cannot specify how children should acquire these skills, but it does demand that they be used in a variety of contexts for a range of purposes and audiences.

These demands are based upon recent work in the general field of literacy which suggests that, for teachers concerned with developing the literacy of their pupils, the major task is to provide appropriate contexts for that development. The features of these contexts have been expressed in terms of a set of 'conditions for learning' (Cambourne, 1988), prominent among which are opportunities to learn through progressive approximations to literate behaviour in a responsive, 'scaffolded' environment. Applying these ideas to writing, it has begun to seem that the teaching of writing is largely about getting the context right. It is tempting to assume that if the optimum classroom context could be established, this would in itself lead to an improved product and process in children's writing.

Such an assumption leaves the problem of determining just what the best context for writing is. Theories of which factors in context are important are as yet undeveloped. It has tended to be assumed that such context-producing teaching strategies as conferencing, drafting, collaboration and revising have a beneficial effect upon writing but we have yet to formalise a theory to explain why this should be true and just how, and indeed if, these factors help. The work described in this paper is a small part of a much large study into these issues.

Describing the context of classroom writing

To start to develop a theory about such issues we need, firstly, to decide just what constitutes the context of children's writing. The common-sense approach to this

might be to list all the factors which seem to impinge upon the child writer as he/she works on a piece of writing in school. This listing might include such factors as:
- school and county policies on teaching writing,
- recent in-service work in the school, or undertaken by a particular teacher,
- the teacher's views about writing and the learning of writing,
- the setting in which writing takes place, including the social and physical organisation of the classroom,
- the range of writing that a child has experienced in the past,
- the nature and range of the audiences for which the child has written,
- the teacher's intended outcome for a specific piece of writing,
- the intended outcome of the child for that piece of writing,
- any intervention by the teacher in the form of task description and subsequent response to the outcome,
- the subject, genre, purpose and audience of each particular piece.

This provides a complex web of contextual factors which are interrelated and may be differentially perceived by the participants in the process, namely teachers and children.

The operation of contextual factors

In order to investigate the operation of this web of factors, a number of case studies were undertaken into the contexts provided for children's writing in primary classrooms. Each case study focused upon the work over a period of one term (approximately twelve weeks) of one lower junior classroom. The schools were selected from a range of schools which had recently undertaken a school-based in-service programme on writing. The classes were run by teachers selected as successful in the teaching of writing by the head teacher of those schools. Each case involved study at several levels:
- the teachers were interviewed to ascertain their general approaches to writing in the class, and to establish their aims and intentions for the particular writing tasks which they set or encouraged.
- two children in each class were selected and interviewed to establish both their general views about writing and their perceptions about particular writing tasks.
- copies of the writing of these two children, at various stages of development, were collected over the case study period.
- a range of writing sessions were observed (by tape recording and extensive field notes) and discussed with the children.
- parents were visited and interviewed about their children's experiences of writing, and the children asked to keep writing diaries to include home-based activities over a two week period.

Naturally, the study produced a great deal of data, including pieces of writing, transcripts of interviews and observation notes, and much of this remains to be analysed in detail. I shall here report only on some of the broad implications which have begun to emerge. I shall attempt to contrast some of the findings from two of the classes in order to sketch some of the similarities and differences of context and the implications of these findings for the teaching of writing.

These two classes were studied during the second term of the children's 4th primary year. Class A (whose teacher I shall refer to as Mr Jones) can be termed a "traditional" writing class, whilst class B (whose teacher I shall refer to as Mrs Evans) is an example of a "process writing' class.

The traditional class

This class was described by its teacher as a secure environment for work, in which children knew what was expected and received praise for effort. The teacher was most concerned to match the work to the children's level of attainment and felt writing tasks were ideal as "they can be tackled at any level". Mr Jones recognised that the children wrote in a number of subjects, but said that it was essential to practise writing for itself, particularly if new skills such as drafting were to be mastered. He felt under pressure to introduce a drafting approach, but said that on the whole he already encouraged the children to check their spellings before submitting work for marking. He felt that the ability to reshape the content of the story was probably beyond the abilities of children of this age.

English tasks consisted mainly of short answer or cloze-based scheme work with a creative writing session each week. The teacher would assign a title from a list of ideas which had been successfully used before. The children also retold a bible story each week, wrote a report of a science lesson and did short answer work for history and geography.

There was a low hum of activity and children talked, mainly about work-centred issues. If the noise level rose the teacher would call out a name and the class would instantly become quiet. Work was collected by a named individual at the end of each session. The work was marked, mainly for transcription details and returned, sometimes with a verbal or written comment.

The process writing class

Mrs Evans described her class as 'a context for learning about the writing process, a garden of opportunities'. She stated that she wanted her children to become independent learners and support each other in learning the craft of writing. She was very enthusiastic about the writing process and committed to giving the children every possible support in learning to revise and edit their work. She gave a high profile to literacy activities and had provided a comfortable, well stocked reading area and plenty of teacher-made posters on the wall emphasising various aspects of literacy and children's individual achievements.

Writing tasks were usually related to topic work or literature and most writing was done into rough books to be recopied later into the appropriate exercise book or onto paper. Most, but not all drafted work reached a finished stage. The teacher allocated the tasks, although not all children did the same tasks. Children were keen to have their work chosen for "publication" in class books and displays. The children in this class generally worked round their home table, but did not have fixed places and sat with friends. Privacy was available for those who preferred it.

Contrasts and Similarities

As the study progressed it became clear that there were striking differences between the contexts in both classes and also unexpected similarities. There were, of course, examples from children in both classes of excellent writing, very appropriate to its purpose and audience, and others which were obviously not so well thought out, but it was difficult to link this variation infallibly to particular elements of the context of either class.

Although both teachers had recently participated in prolonged in-service work about writing, they had each reached very different conclusions about its teaching. They differed in the ways in which they talked about writing. For example, Mr Jones talked about writing as a skill learnt through practice and felt that the weekly 'creative writing' session was essential practice for becoming a mature writer. He expressed the belief that other types of writing should be taught, for example, letter writing, but that this could be satisfactorily dealt with through exercises. Mrs Evans also stressed that children need to practice writing but she emphasised that her children needed to practice a range of writing skills which could only be done through experience of a range of types of writing. The manner and degree to which these expressed beliefs were realised as classroom practice differed in each class. For example, on a number of occasions Mrs Evans expressed concern with audience and purpose and specifically structured writing tasks to focus upon these aspects. However, her notions of audience and purpose were not shared by the children, who still seemed to feel that they were writing for the teacher but that the rules had changed slightly. This was clearly seen on one occasion when the children were asked to write thank-you letters to the local vicar who had shown them around his church. She gave a full introduction to the whole class, discussing the purpose of the letter and the content and language which might be used. Talking to the children during their writing of these letters, however, it became clear that they were more concerned with "what Miss told us to write" and whether they would meet her criteria about length and spelling than with the needs of the vicar as a audience. In fact a number did not remember that the letters were intended for the vicar. Some were not sure whether they would actually be sent at all. It is doubtful, therefore, whether in cases such as this the intended audience and purpose were actually part of the context for writing as perceived by the children.

The ways the children discussed the writing process also differed, but not directly according to their situation or the teacher's instruction. Mr Jones placed a strong emphasis upon neatness and accuracy and would mention these qualities in every introduction to a writing task. Both the studied children in this class, however, seemed, on occasion, to go beyond the emphases of their teacher and talked about the writing process in terms of content, revision and audience as well as neatness and accuracy. In one instance a girl in class A attributed to her teacher critical facilities about writing he actually showed no evidence of possessing. She suggested that in writing, "You have to have the right ideas and they have got to be interesting. You can put stuff in to make it longer but that isn't really ideas and Sir'll know." Mr Jones was flattered, but agreed that the child was going "beyond her teaching" in the sense that he had never discussed these aspects.

The similarities between the two classes were also notable. In discussing the features of writing products the children in the traditional class usually prioritised neatness and accuracy. However in the process writing class the children were also very concerned about the length of writing and neatness of work, although these were aspects that the teacher was keen to play down. Mrs Evans's continual stress on rough work, and disregard for correct spelling in preliminary drafts seemed to have had little effect. Not surprisingly, this was a source of some frustration to the teacher who felt that her children were bound to be used to traditional school demands and it would take some time before her new demands resulted in a change of perceptions.

Looking at a number of discussions with members of both classes, it seems that there were implicit rules for writing which were recognised by the children. These show a surprisingly high degree of similarity from class to class.

Context as individual

These observations seem to call for a re-evaluation of the notion of context and a shift in a theoretical conceptualisation of contexts for writing. It may be that the whole idea of context as a set of identifiable factors acting upon the individual is inadequate and it may be more helpful, in fact, to consider context as mental, that is as not having an external existence identifiable to an observer. Context is, according to Mercer (1990), "everything that the participants know and understand (over and above that which is explicit in what they say) which they use to make sense of what is said and done" (p. 31) . This is further elaborated: "What counts for context for learners, as for analytic linguists, is whatever they consider relevant." (Mercer, 1992, p.31). If this is the case then the contextual factors described earlier do not exist in an objective sense. They are only given meaning to the extent to which they are perceived as important by the participants. It is clear that these perceptions of the participants are not simply derived from any current experiences, but are a product of these experiences and previous experiences, the effects of which continue to reverberate for a considerable time.

Context as culture

Whilst the differences in context perceived by individuals may lead us to consider context as mental it is also worth noting the high level of similarity between the understandings of children in the same class and in some cases between all the children. The tape transcripts, field notes and photographs reveal that each classroom had a unique culture - with values, norms, beliefs and organisational structures. This appears as a set of shared understandings to which none of the participants explicitly shows adherence, yet in the light of which each acts.

The children seemed able to incorporate new rules into this system. In the process writing class the teacher produced a range of notices on the walls of the classroom about the various stages of writing. Then children were given the opportunity to discuss which processes would be suitable for a particular task. The teacher was at pains to talk to the children about the stages. This was not, however, reflected in the children's discussions. They referred to the stages they had discussed as a rule system which applied to the writing they did in this class (but not in other classes and not at home). They did not consider that the writing task they engaged in should influence the stages they would use although the teacher had explicitly told them that it might. It seemed as if one rule system had been substituted for another without any apparent increase in the children's levels of awareness about writing processes.

As mentioned above, Mrs Evans was most concerned to provide authentic audiences and purposes for her children so that they could be involved in 'real' writing. Their discussions, however, seemed to indicate that they continued to view these as school tasks, primarily done for the teacher. Questions about ownership further supported this impression, as the children in the process class did not feel that the work was theirs, whilst on some occasions a child in the traditional class expressed strong ownership of stories she had written.

Thus in both these classes there was a strong culture in the sense of a set of social norms, rituals, conduct rules and meaning systems, which was clearly a school culture. Within these classes the rules and meaning systems about writing were school rules and meanings about the activity of writing in school - a process seen as different from writing at home, and as Neisser (1976) suggests, it is not unusual for children to "leave their life situations at the door" in approaching school tasks. Moreover, the rules in both classes showed a very high degree of similarity, despite the very different conceptions of writing held by the teachers. The process writing teacher was keen to talk about this. She felt that she had done all the right things to change the way children wrote, but realised that they had not gained the insights into the writing processes she had expected.

Context as control

In a general sense it is obvious that the context of all writing is socially shaped. All writers write for socially significant audiences and purposes and the genres they use reflect relationships between individuals and socially agreed conventions of style. School writing, therefore, has particular features shaped by its social setting. The context of any piece of writing can be considered as whatever the individual perceives to be relevant to the task of producing it. In the classroom the major part of these perceptions stem from the rules, norms and accepted practices of writing which form part of the prevailing culture in that class. What is striking is the fact that in this study it seemed that children's perceptions of these features were broadly similar across classes, even where one teacher had deliberately tried to change the children's understandings about writing.

It seems that this teacher's attempted introduction of real purposes and audiences for the children in her class had not really changed her children's perceptions of the audiences for whom they were writing. Given this, therefore, it might be thought reasonable to expect that the children would apply the understandings of writing and the writing processes with which they were familiar. The rules about writing might have changed as the teacher tried to introduce a process writing model, but as the classroom culture was essentially unchanged, then new understandings about writing did not need to be generated.

The key to the problem raised here may be to do with the concept of authenticity in classroom writing. Authentic audiences and purposes are not necessarily those provided by the teacher, however real the teacher may consider them to be. Authenticity of task needs to be recognised by an individual within the classroom culture. In assigning "real" tasks to the children, teachers may unwittingly change them into teacher-set tasks which are no more authentic than traditional imaginative writing exercises. In the classrooms examined in this study the audiences and purposes for writing were largely teacher dominated because they originated in a teacher controlled curriculum. An authentic task is, by definition, one whose purpose is defined by the author.

In trying to teach children about writing it may therefore be necessary to negotiate new perceptions about writing through renegotiation of the classroom culture. This cannot be done by simply changing one element of the rules. Perhaps what needs to be renegotiated, in order to offer authentic purposes and audiences, is not the rule system, but control of the writing curriculum itself. In UK schools, dominated by a National Curriculum which circumscribes classroom activity, this may be a difficult proposition at the moment. Many teachers are only now becoming familiar with the model of writing this curriculum presents: involving writing skills such as drafting and revising. The fact remains, however, that these skills, introduced in a teacher controlled environment do not seem to produce the revolutionary understandings about writing which were anticipated.

It may be that only in a situation where young writers are able to negotiate tasks for purposes which they can recognise and have some say in, can the classroom culture, and the perceptions and context of the individuals within it, significantly increase young children's understandings about writing. Authorship is, after all, about exercising control over a particular medium to meet specific social demands. The purposes of writing will be dictated by the culture that gives rise to them and the processes for writing will be those agreed as appropriate within that culture. In classrooms there will always be a social context for writing which is formed by, and gives rise to individual contexts for specific writing experiences. Change in the writing demands in a class must be created and recognised by all concerned, and this may involve giving all the participants in the class some control over the curriculum.

References

CAMBOURNE, B. (1988) *The Whole Story* Auckland, NZ: Ashton Scholastic

MERCER, N. (1990) 'Context, continuity and communication in learning', in Potter, F. (ed) *Reading, Learning and Media Education* Oxford: Basil Blackwell

MERCER, N. (1992) 'Culture, context and the construction of knowledge in the classroom', in Light, P. & Butterworth, G. (eds) *Context and cognition* Hemel Hempstead: Harvester Wheatsheaf

NEISSER, U. (1976) 'General, academic and artificial intelligence', in Resnick, L. (ed) *The Nature of Intelligence* London: Chambers/Murray

Fostering Language Awareness Through Language Play

Juliet Partridge

While there is general support for the existence of an important relationship between literacy and language awareness, there is considerable controversy about the relative importance of particular aspects of awareness. Metalinguistic awareness has been viewed from a number of perspectives: as word awareness (Tunmer, Herriman and Nesdale, 1988), phonological awareness (Bryant and Bradley, 1985) or syntactic awareness (Bowey, 1986).

To compare the findings of the major studies is extremely difficult, since not only are different theoretical perspectives on literacy learning evident, but the gathering of information from the children about their awareness shows, in many instances, a lack of consideration for the inherently social interactive nature of language learning, the range of functions of language, and how children learn language.

Word awareness

Several research studies which have focussed on requiring children to segment meaningful utterances into their component words have revealed the difficulty for children in performing this task (Berthoud-Papandropoulou, 1978; Tunmer, Bowey and Grieve, 1983). It does seem to be logical that since written language is recorded in what we loosely term 'words', the beginning reader must develop a sensitivity to the words which make up the speech flow. This is not as straightforward as it appears. Many adults, in fact, often confound word boundaries. A tertiary student wrote 'Bate Hoven's Syntheny' in an essay recently, and 'alot' for ' a lot' is very common. A beginning reader encounters a similar task to an adult listening to a foreign language. While children may be able to isolate and reflect on 'words' in speech which have concrete referents such as table, or shoe, functional words may be dismissed as meaningless. This is apparent from children's writing attempts, when early writing may have similar features as to children's early telegraphic speech.

Read (1978) suggests that words and phonetic segments have some characteristics in common - they both appear to be units accessible to the speaker and both have defied linguistic description. He goes on to define a word as "any segment of a sentence bounded by successive points at which pausing is possible", a definition he admits is somewhat 'lame'. Native speakers of a language can identify words with a considerable degree of consistency, in spite of the difficulty linguists have in defining a word.

For the pre-literate child, words are experienced in the context of other words, with their attention focussed on the meaning, This was shown by Berthoud-Papandropoulou (1978) with children aged 4 years to 12 years. A general developmental trend in linguistic thinking was evident, in the sense of the child's ability to reflect on the nature of language itself. The youngest children, for example, tended to define words in terms of things which have an independent existence. For example, 'strawberry is a word because it grows in the garden'. Long and short words were related to objects with those properties, such as 'train' or "an 'eye' because it's small". Older children tended to define long words in terms of letter length, or to attempt to elongate the acoustic signal by stressing vowels e.g. 'oraaaaaange'. Letters and not sounds were most commonly referred to in relation to the composition of words.

Since the concept 'word' comes from *written* language it is to be expected that only those children who have developed knowledge of the written language would be able to define 'word'. Young children are unable to separate the logical functions of language from its interpersonal functions, to understand that words have no intrinsic relation to the things they stand for. Asked to analyse a spoken string into its component words such as "Six children are playing", the youngest children would be likely to list six children's names to justify their answer of six words.

We do not treat words in speech as individual entities - rather we must discover the grammatical relations between words in order to determine the semantic interpretation. Many schoolchild howlers are a reflection of a lack of knowledge of the grammatical relations and thus lead to a loss of semantic interpretation. The most common examples of this seem to arise in settings where extra-linguistic information is not available. Hymns sung in church without benefit of the written word are often interpreted in unusual ways. For example: *Gladly my cross eyed bear* in place of *Gladly my cross I'd bear*. Naturally children may play on this knowledge in a deliberate fashion, which may show evidence of linguistic awareness.

Tunmer, Herriman and Nesdale (1988) argue also that there is no need to treat word awareness separately from phonological awareness. The ability to segment the spoken word 'dog' for example, into its constituent phonemic elements indicates that a child is able to dissociate the phonological realisation of the word from its referent. Tunmer and his colleagues also propose that the ability to reflect on phonemes presupposes the ability to reflect on words. In other words, phonological awareness develops after word awareness. In measuring phonological awareness, however, Tunmer and his colleagues created non-digraph, non-word syllables. The ability to segment strings of nonsense words does not have any real language function, and it is difficult to know how this reflects children's awareness of linguistic structure. Work by Fox and Routh (1975) showed more promise. They devised a way of eliciting information from children that did not require the use of metalinguistic terms such as word. Children were asked to give progressively smaller bits of sentences. It was found that children as young as four could break sentences into words and syllables. Whether this can be deemed conscious linguistic awareness is, however, still debatable, especially since the experimenter determined when the child had sufficiently analysed the sentence, and rewarded him with a raisin!

The evidence suggests that a pre-literate child's grasp of 'word' in the spoken language may be embryonic. In part this is because the word has no reality in spoken language.

Phonological awareness

This particular area of linguistic awareness has received the most attention in experimental studies. The reasons for this could relate either to a perceived ease of accessibility to sound features, or the belief that beginning readers need to have awareness in this area as a priority. There tends to be support for the child's awareness of phonemes as a necessary concomitant of reading acquisition (Liberman, 1982; Tunmer, 1986).

Phonological awareness can be described as:
(a) awareness of the different sounds of the language
(b) knowing how these sounds are combined to form words of the language and
(c) knowing how specific individual words are similar or different in terms of their sound structure.

We speak in continuous acoustic strings. We do not articulate separate sounds one after the other, but rather overlap them. For example, the /d/ in dim and doom cannot be separated from the vowel following, and in fact, the /d/ is articulated quite differently in each case. In other words, speech sounds vary according to their phonological environments, which can be determined by their position in a syllable, the stress and the adjacent sounds.

Young children are obviously sensitive to the differences in phonemes as they can respond to such tasks as selecting a hat from a cat, but the awareness of these differences in phonemes is not explicit. We can compare our ability to crawl, but our inability to describe the actual crawling process.

The main question which puzzles researchers is whether phonological awareness precedes reading acquisition, or whether as a result of learning to read the child develops a conscious awareness of the phonological system. Bradley and Bryant (1983) produced the first empirical evidence of a causal link between phonological awareness and reading, dmonstrating a link between pre-school ability to recognise rhyme and alliteration and children's later spelling and reading achievements. Rhyming and alliteration in particular give children experience in breaking words into phonetic segments and of grouping together words which are very different from each other but that do have phonetic segments in common (Bradley and Bryant, 1985). It is suggested that research needs to be carried out into the role of parents in fostering the child's rhyming ability and play with sounds. It is evident from Bryant and Bradley's studies that children do take to rhyme and alliteration before they go to school, but it is not clear in what ways parents may actively encourage or discourage this aspect of language development.

Manipulating the phonemes in words is very difficult for young children, especially pre-literates. Some of the tests given to young children, such as phoneme substitution, require a number of different processes, drawing heavily on short term memory and abstraction (Bruce 1964). The substitution of phonemes occurs naturally in producing rhymes. However, while young children enjoy repeating rhymes and hearing them read aloud they can often find it quite difficult to produce a rhyme themselves. The production of rhymes 'inadvertently' in their speech play is common, but asking children to find a word that rhymes with another appears to be drawing on the conscious awareness level.

The writer, together with a group of Year 4 Early Childhood pre-service teachers, was interested in finding out how children respond to phonemic awareness tasks, and compiled a list of tasks, selected and modified from some of those used in the studies discussed earlier in this chapter, to be used in a one-to-one situation with children aged 4 years to 7 years.

Tasks 1 and 2 involved children in determining which of two spoken words was longer or shorter. The same words were used in each task, but in reverse order. No suggestions were offered as to what longer or short meant, although a practice task was included. Results across the tasks were inconsistent. If a child had determined that a word was longer in the first task, he might deem it shorter in the second. It is not clear on what basis the children conceived 'length' but whatever their initial hypothesis, whether on the basis of syllables, phonemes or letters, many children did not maintain it.

Task 3 involved children in identifying a word after removing a prefix, suffix, initial or final consonant. It was found that removal of suffixes and prefixes was the easiest, followed by final and initial consonant removal. Medial consonants were the most difficult. Some responses reveal that the children were trying to make sense of a task which is essentially totally meaningless. *Sadness* minus *ness* produced the response of *still sad* from one five year old, and *netball* from a six year old.

Task 4 required the addition of a suffix, prefix, initial or final consonant. This was found to be easier than the deletion task but still engendered some interesting responses. One child believed that *grate* plus *ful* equals food, while *birth* plus *day* equals happy.

Task 5 required the substitution of phonemes and this was found to be the most difficult task across all age groups. The addition of sounds to the original word was quite common e.g. sblack, cryt. Some of these responses are words that children would immediately reject in their spoken language on the basis of their implicit linguistic knowledge. As noted earlier, the adults performing these tasks were very reliant on their knowledge of the written forms.

Task 6 required the children to select the 'odd man out' in a set of three words, two of which rhymed. While this task was the easiest for all groups it still brought forth some interesting responses, e.g. **key shoe too**. *Shoe is odd because it has to go on your foot.*

It was found by most of the adults carrying out these tasks that the children became very tired, and it was hard to get them to respond. None of the 4 year old children could cope with Task 5 at all. Many of the children were somewhat disturbed, despite reassurances that this was not a test. One child even burst into tears. The tasks themselves bear no resemblance to anything that the child actually does when engaging in real literacy events. There is a tendency in these 'testing' situations to confuse the child's linguistic 'knowing' with his performance. Most children are very aware of the strange situations that occur in schools, and are prepared to humour adults. One 5 year old child decided not to be implicated in any way, and gave a false name!

"We are still left with the need to elucidate why the over-seven-year-old can ignore his speech act knowledge and give the disembedded, abstract responses which adults tend to give. Something rather deep must change around seven years, which would explain why somewhat contrived experimental questions finally do get the 'right' cognitive response, albeit often accompanied by a smile or a shrug of the shoulders, as if to show that the child realises that speech act conventions are being violated" (Karmiloff-Smith, 1980, p.225).

Syntactic Awareness

Bowey (1986) suggests that relatively little research has dealt with children's awareness of grammatical well-formedness, although attempts to elicit acceptability judgements from very young children were carried out up to 20 years ago. Eliciting children's acceptability judgements is fraught with difficulties. Children tend to respond to the semantic content rather than syntactic considerations. For example, Gleitman et al. (1972) asked children to judge a sentence 'good' or 'silly', which naturally led to children deciding on the basis of content - a silly sentence may be *John has not got a sister* - because their friend John has got a sister.

There are important changes between the ages of four and eight, and further progress towards adult levels throughout the primary school, in terms of children's awareness of sentence structure, which is a reflection of an ability to shift attention from the meaning of sentences and their associated context to the linguistic forms themselves (Ryan and Ledger, 1984). Appropriate experiences with print undoubtedly play an important role in the development of conscious awareness. Cognitive and linguistic maturity are not the sole determinants of growth.

The questions one asks children about such knowledge are critical. Access to what children are aware of, and what they know about both the structure and function of their language has been seriously impaired by the ways in which this information has been solicited (Clark 1978). For example, Bowey (1986) required his subjects in one experiment to repeat grammatically deviant sentences, and in the next to correct errors in grammatically deviant sentences.

A study of children's corrections of errors in grammatically deviant sentences, using two puppets, was carried out by the writer with a group of five and six year olds. It was found that in correcting the errors the children tended to stress words preceding or following, while still producing the corrected form. Given the example - *Sandra is paint a picture*, stress would be given to the *is* as in *Sandra is painting a picture*.

There is little dispute that interaction with written language requires metalinguistic awareness, and that certain kinds of metalinguistic awareness develop through interaction with written language, but it is argued here that many of the experimental studies discussed earlier are not assessing what metalinguistic awareness the child possesses, but rather trying to make their implicit knowledge explicit. All adults know how to order a group of adjectives in front of a noun, but only linguistics can define explicitly the rules that we all implicitly know.

Donaldson (1978) comments that very rarely do children ask questions about language, even when it is evident that the language is unfamiliar, and this is particularly true when children listen to stories. They may ask many questions about characters, motives, and structure of the plot, but they hardly ever focus their attention on the language used.

If true, this suggests that it may be interesting to consider some ways in which children could be encouraged to develop awareness of language. Some aspects of language play will now be discussed in order to assess their contribution to the child's development of awareness of language structure.

The role of language play

Language play combines many aspects of the child's increasing command of language structure and function. One of the first kinds of play is evident in the way that the sounds of language are manipulated. Chukovsky (1968) claims that it would be difficult to find a more useful phonetic exercise than the rhyming of nonsense syllables that the child tirelessly and effortlessly produces; even before the age of one year children amuse themselves by endless rhythmic jabbering, repeating again and again some favourite sound.

Adults play a significant role in helping their children develop this sensitivity to sound, rhyme and rhythm of language. A baby inspires an adult to blossom forth into raptures of meaningless nonsense, which is generally rhyming and rhythmic. One father was heard to chant "Pippy, poppy pooh pa poing pong pants" several times while hugging, tickling and kissing his young baby. There was much variation in each repetition in terms of speed, rising and falling tones, and the accompanying non-verbal behaviours. The baby obviously enjoyed every minute of it. The strong use of alliteration and the plosive /p/ is common in these early sensory language plays. Very few such chants would make use of /h/ or a vowel. One may argue that language play may be influenced by phonological features. Nursery rhymes, a tradition in most languages, are an extremely rich source of phonological contrasts and similarities.

There can be little disagreement that playing with sounds from the very beginning of language use helps children to develop an awareness of sound patterns and the ability to rhyme, which Bryant and Bradley (1985) believe to be causal in learning to read. Children's energy and exuberance are closely tied to linguistic outpourings. Jumping, hopping, skipping and clapping seem to call for the accompaniment of rhythmic rhymes. These are often dependent on strong syllable clusters although it is unlikely that children at this stage are conscious of the syllable as a linguistic phenomenon.

The use of 'topsy turvies' as described by Chukovsky (1968) gives further access to children's increasing knowledge of the world, and evidence that children are starting to manipulate the language, using it as an object for its own sake. Topsy-turvies turn word meanings upside down and are quite common in nursery rhymes. Children are manipulating the language at the semantic level. Chukovsky describes his two year old daughter's invention of 'oggie-miaow', her deliberate attempt to sever the tie between object and its regular function, as play of a very special kind.

Play as it is experienced in any other type of game is accepted by the child voluntarily as self-deception, and the more self-deception is involved, the more attractive is the game. In topsy-turvies the situation is completely opposite - the play is enjoyed to the extend that there is awareness of the self-deception; recognising this awareness takes first importance (Chukovsky, 1968). This is an interesting observation and lends further support to the idea that linguistic awareness might have strong roots in language development well before schooling and literacy intervene.

The universality of language play in children's language development suggests that it has an important role in helping the child grasp the intricacies of the linguistic system. It also suggests that children are interested and fascinated by language itself.

All language play reveals the child's implicit knowledge of the syntactic system but it is not until the child begins to play with riddles that evidence of ability to manipulate syntactic structure is apparent. Riddles develop late, and are a complex form of language play. Bowes (1979) found in her studies of Year 1 children, and their riddle knowledge, that those children who could tell riddles were more linguistically aware in other dimensions, particularly in understanding ambiguity and figurative language. Sanches and Kirschen-Gimblett (1976) collected examples of speech play from children of 5 to 14 years of age, and suggested that a progression through phonological, grammatical, semantic and ultimately sociolinguistic levels of language play was evident in children's use of riddles. A similar sequence through phonological to sociolinguistic appears to be operating in terms of children's language play before school.

It is possible then to have children exhibiting phonological play in all levels of awareness. While the baby may just be repeating pleasant sounds, the older child will be deliberately using the sounds of the language for functional reasons. Factor (1988) provides the following humorous example of an older child's tongue twister, a phonological play with intent to shock. "I slit a sheet. A sheet I slit. Upon the slitted sheet I sit."

Not all of the child's language play before school revolves around oral language, however. Story reading and telling is a major part of most children's pre-school lives and there is evidence that language play is further stimulated through the child's encounters with literature. Language play may be considered in literary terms in relation to nursery rhymes and other verse, riddles, puns, and play on ambiguity. Lindfors (1987) suggests that it is the unexpected in the language of such books that is most engaging.

Children's language play before school, therefore, seems to contain all the features of the language which they need to use in school, particularly in embracing literacy. The child may have played with the phonology, the syntactic and the semantic elements. It also shows that the child progresses from the unconscious stage of language awareness to the more sophisticated analytical stages. This kind of play must be considered as critical to the development of more abstract understanding, i.e. to the use of metalanguage. Language play, it is proposed, is a necessary part of the scaffold to the child's conscious awareness, when those forms and functions he has 'playfully' manipulated, can be dealt with in more abstract ways.

References

BERTHOUD-PAPANDROPOULOU, I. (1978) 'An experimental study of children's ideas about language', in Sinclair, A., Jarvella, R.J. and Level, W.J.M. (eds) *The Child's Conception of Language* Springer-Verlag: Berlin

BOWES, J. (1979) Children's language play and awareness of language: some possible relationships to reading *Working Papers in Language and Linguistics*, 9, pp. 42-61

BOWEY, J. (1986) 'Syntactic awareness and verbal performance from preschool to fifth grade' *Journal of Psycholinguistic Research* 15 (4), pp. 285-308.

BRADLEY L. & BRYANT, P.E. (1983) 'Categorizing sounds and learning to read - a causal connection' *Nature* 301, pp. 419-421

BRADLEY, L. & BRYANT, P.E. (1985) *Rhyme and Reason in Reading and Spelling*. Michigan: University of Michigan Press

BRUCE, D. (1964) 'An analysis of word sounds by young children' *British Journal of Educational Psychology* 34, pp. 158-170.

BRYANT, P. & BRADLEY, L. (1985) *Children's Reading Problems* Oxford: Blackwell

CHUKOVSKY, K. (1968) *From Two to Five*. Berkeley: University of California Press

CLARK, E. (1978) 'Awareness of language: some evidence from what children say and do', in Sinclair, A., Jarvella, R.J. and Level, W.J.M. (eds) *The Child's Conception of Language* Springer-Verlag: Berlin

DONALDSON, M. (1978) *Children's Minds* London: Fontana

FACTOR, J. (1988) *Captain Cook Chased a Chool* Melbourne: Penguin Books.

FOX, B. & ROUTH, D.K. (1975) 'Analysing spoken language into words, syllables and phonemes: a developmental study', *Journal of Psycholinguistic Research*, 4, pp. 331-342

GLEITMAN, L.R., GLEITMAN, H. & SHIPLEY, E.F. (1972) 'The emergence of the child as grammarian', *Cognition*, 1, pp. 137-164

KARMILOFF-SMITH, A. (1980) Review of *Children's Minds, Journal of Child Language*, 7, pp. 223-227

LIBERMAN, I.Y. (1982) 'A language oriented view of reading and its disabilities', in Mykelbust, H. (ed.) *Progress in Learning Disabilities* New York: Grune and Stratton

LINDFORS, J. (1987) *Children's Language and Learning* Englewood Cliffs, New Jersey: Prentice-Hall

READ, C. (1978) 'Children's awareness of language, with emphasis on sound systems', in Sinclair, A., Jarvella, R.J. and Level, W.J.M. (eds) *The Child's Conception of Language* Springer-Verlag: Berlin

RYAN, E. & LEDGER, G.W. (1984) 'Learning to attend to sentence structure; links between metalinguistic development and reading', in Downing, J. and Valtin, R. (eds) *Language Awareness and Learning to Read* New York: Springer-Verlag

SANCHES, M. & KIRSHENBLATT-GIMBLETT, B. (1976) 'Children's traditional speech play and child language' in Kirshenblatt-Gimblett, B. (ed.) *Speech Play* Pennsylvania: University of Pennsylvania

TUNMER, W. (1986) 'Misconceptions about reading', *Education* 35 (1), pp. 13-15

TUNMER, W., BOWEY, J. & GRIEVE, R. (1983) 'The development of young children's awareness of the word as a unit of spoken language', *Journal of Psycholinguistic Research*, 12 (6), pp. 567-594

TUNMER, W., HERRIMAN, M. & NESDALE, A. (1988) 'Metalinguistic abilities and beginning reading', *Reading Research Quarterly* 23 (2), pp. 134-158

Assessment as a Context for Literacy Development

Christine H. Leland

Introduction

Recently the topic of literacy assessment has been receiving a great deal of negative attention. On the one hand, critics of education loudly lament falling test scores and blame teachers and students alike for not working harder to achieve better results. On the other hand, more and more educators criticize tests that are incongruous with their beliefs about how children learn, and that do not reflect what they are teaching in their classrooms. It seems that everyone is unhappy; some because they perceive that students and teachers are doing an inadequate job, others because they feel trapped by having to be accountable to inadequate assessment measures. The students are at the center of the unhappiness, frustrated and bored by incessant testing that seems to be largely unconnected to what they are doing in or out of school.

MORE is not always BETTER

The malaise that hangs over the assessment issue is compounded by the fact that improvement in education is often equated with an increase in testing. Bintz & Harste (1991) call it "the Miss Piggy philosophy that says 'more is better'" (p. 223). In the U.S., President Bush has repeatedly called for an increase in testing as a way to improve education. Responding to this policy, Goodman wrote as follows in his "Open Letter to President Bush" (1991):

"My teacher colleagues were amazed that the most specific proposal you have made is for the imposition of another new test. Mr. President, had you asked any students, parents or teachers in this country they could have told you that if there is one thing American education does not need it is another test. Our pupils are the most test-abused in the world . . . Furthermore, you and those who put together your proposals seem unaware that the whole concept of how we evaluate in our schools is under intense scrutiny in North America and other parts of the world. Standardized multiple choice tests have been seen to be part of the problem rather than the solution. They provide little useful information for planning instruction or improving schools and they have a built-in, research-demonstrated bias against minority groups, poor people, and creative non-conformists." (p. 1)

According to Clay (1990), the situation is similar elsewhere:

"Recent moves to reform educational administration in Britain, Australia, and New

Zealand have been accompanied by calls for more testing. There is an assumption that giving tests will, ipso facto, improve teaching and learning. However, standardized test scores are only outcome measures. They do not tell us what kinds of teaching to engage in to change those outcomes" (p. 289).

The context of assessment

If *more* testing is not going to improve the dissatisfaction with assessment, then perhaps better testing will. Testing would be better if it helped students and teachers by providing a context for literacy development. Webster's New Collegiate Dictionary (1980) provides the following definition of context: the interrelated conditions in which something exists or occurs, environment. In order for assessment to become a context for literacy development, then it must do more than collect data about how many correct answers a student can choose: it must provide an environment in which learning can take place.

In the past, it seems, we have paid little attention to the concept of context in relation to literacy assessment. Maybe we were bedazzled by the impressive claims of the professional test makers. After all, they boasted that their tests were "objective" and "reliable," and this made many educators afraid to question them. It is possible that the scientific aura surrounding commercial standardized tests has done much to overshadow the simple fact that they do not, in fact, provide a context, an environment, for literacy development. They do not help students to learn, or teachers to teach. Theoretically, test scores should assist teachers in planning future instruction, but more often, the information gained from large-scale testing is used to place children into high and low reading groups, academic and non-academic tracks, and eventually, different professions and occupations.

The issue of validity

It is also conceivable that we have never spent much time thinking about the context of literacy assessment because our approach to literacy instruction has been so narrow. In basal-based (or "scheme"-based) classrooms where isolated students spend a great deal of time drilling on isolated skills, testing the mastery of these skills might appear to be reasonable. If one accepts the notion that test validity refers to the question of whether the test matches what has been taught and how it has been taught (Calfee & Hiebert, 1991), then our present form of standardized assessment appears to be valid in some instances.

Whole language educators, however, maintain that standardized tests can never be valid in their classrooms because they do not measure what has been taught there. First, students in whole language classrooms are taught to ask their own questions and to generate their own answers to those questions. They are not taught to select the best of someone else's answers to someone else's questions. Second, whole language educators reject the belief that literacy is learned as a collection of separate hierarchical skills that can be tested individually. Rather, literacy is thought to be acquired holistically through meaningful exchanges with literate people and through a variety of experiences in a print-rich environment. Whole authentic texts are the focus of instruction, and extensive reading, discussion, and written response to literature are important classroom activities. Third, whole language philosophy stresses the importance of understanding literacy acquisition as a social activity. Literacy development and the assessment of literacy development are viewed from a whole language perspective as social transactions. Therefore, the conventional understanding of assessment as a solitary endeavour where students work with no assistance from teacher or peers is rejected.

Assessment and conversation

According to Satterly (1989), the word 'assessment' is derived from the Latin word *assidere*, which means to sit beside. As Satterly reminds us, "sitting beside children suggests a close relationship and a sharing of experience" (p. 3). Therefore, he finds it ironic (even with due allowance for the ways in which word meanings change over time) that educational assessment is currently associated in many people's minds with objectivity, which he translates as a concentration on measuring discrete skills, and a way to sort children out according to their ability. Whole language educators urge us to discard both of these interpretations and go back to the meaning of the Latin word. From their perspective, assessment needs to be based on sitting beside students and engaging them in conversations about what they have learned, and where we might be able to help them learn more. In conversation, assessment becomes a process of learners working together to generate and answer their own questions. Some of the questions they might ask include: What have I learned? How did I learn it? Is there anything still not clear that I need to learn more about? According to Bintz and Harste (1991), this approach encourages students to "use themselves as a research instrument, and to use assessment as a tool for outgrowing their present selves" (p. 240).

The notion of assessment through conversation is supported by social-constructivist theory which "makes a compelling case for a view of knowledge based on consensus" (McCarthey & Raphael, 1992, p. 20). According to this perspective, "there is no objective reality that can be measured or mirrored" (p. 16); therefore, the pursuit of objectivity in assessment is both unnecessary and unwise. Rather, it is more important to understand assessment in a new context. Instead of seeing assessment as a way to check up on students and to put them into groups based on ability, we should view assessment as a way to establish and maintain dialogue in a community of learners.

Paris, Lawton, Turner & Roth (1991) refer to dialogue-based assessment as "a developmental model" and argue that it provides "opportunities that are intrinsically motivating for students. Activities that invoke intrinsic motivation often contain elements of challenge and curiosity" (p. 19). This approach encourages students to set and meet their own goals rather than competing with others for high test scores. Through dialogue, both student and teacher become active participants in the assessment process. "Dialogues between teachers and students should be used to set standards and evaluate progress. When students become participants in the process of ongoing assessment, they can adopt personal mastery goals" and assessment can serve genuine motivational purposes like it does for athletes and musicians (p. 19).

Dynamic assessment

One way to maximize the role of conversation in assessment is through the use of a dynamic assessment mode. This type of assessment focuses on providing support for the student during the testing session. Instead of finding out what the student cannot do (as in the standardized testing mode), the object is to discover the conditions under which s/he can learn successfully. According to Lidz (1987), "two words are of primary importance to the definition and conceptualisation of dynamic assessment: activity and modifiability" (p. 3). The first term refers to the active role taken by both the examiner and the learner. The examiner actively intervenes in the assessment process by prodding, directing, and reinforcing the learner to become an "active seeker and organizer of information" (pp. 3-4). The second term (modifiability) refers to the changes in cognitive functioning that are induced by the interaction between the examiner and the learner. The modifiability of intelligence has been studied by Feuerstein (1980) and his colleagues in their work with low-ability Israeli students. By working with the students during the assessment process, these researchers were able to improve the students' general cognitive functioning. "The gains they documented for mentally retarded students have put into question notions that intelligence is static and unchanging" (Brozo, 1990, p. 523).

The theoretical foundation for dynamic assessment can be found in Vygotsky's notion that learning is socially mediated, and that more knowledgeable members of a culture can help less knowledgeable members learn. "Vygotskian perspectives suggest that students learn ... through interaction with a more knowledgeable adult or peer" (McCarthey & Raphael, 1992, p. 17). Of particular importance are the modelling and thinking aloud done by the more expert person. Campione & Brown (1987) describe what happens during dynamic assessment as follows:

142

"At the outset, the child and an adult work together, with the adult doing most of the work and serving as an expert model. As the child acquires some degree of skill, the adult cedes the child responsibility for part of the job and does less of the work. Gradually, the child takes more of the initiative, and the adult serves primarily to provide support and help when the child experiences problems. Eventually, the child internalises the initially joint activities and becomes capable of carrying them out independently. At the outset, the adult is the model, critic, and interrogator, leading the child toward expertise; at the end, the child adopts these self-regulation and self-interrogation roles. It is this gradual transfer of control that we seek to capture in our assessment and instructional sessions" (p.83).

In this model, the teacher is working within what Vygotsky (1962) called the zone of proximal development. This concept refers to the difference between what a learner can achieve on his or her own, and what that same learner can accomplish with the help of a more advanced learner, typically the teacher. According to Vygotsky (1978), assessment should help to identify "those functions that have not yet matured but are in the process of maturation, functions that will mature tomorrow but are in the embryonic stage. These functions could be called the 'buds' or 'flowers' rather than the fruits of development" (pp. 86-87). By contrast, traditional assessment measures what has already been fully developed, not what is in the process of developing.

In dynamic assessment, the teacher's role in judging and facilitating student achievement is greatly expanded over what it was in the traditional testing mode. Instead of filling the role of a technician who administers a test that was designed by someone else far removed from the classroom, the teacher is now responsible for evaluating and responding to the needs of individual students "on a moment to moment basis" (Johnston, 1987). When this occurs, assessment and instruction become two sides of the same process. According to Brozo (1990), assessment is then valid because it not only reflects classroom instruction, but becomes an essential part of it. "When testing and teaching become integral events, the assessment process looks very much like a well planned reading lesson" (p. 522). Cioffi & Carney (1983) describe a dynamic reading assessment in which the child is told that he will receive help if has difficulty with some of the words.

"When Peter misreads *slice*, for example, the examiner isolates the phonogram *ice*, which Peter pronounces correctly, then calls Peter's attention to the initial consonant blend *sl*. Peter is asked if he knows words beginning with *sl*; he gives some examples. Then he blends the initial *sl* with the *ice*" (p.766).

Although this procedure is contrary to standard administration protocols, it "reveals the kinds of instruction he should receive" (p. 768) in order to be successful in reading. If standard administration procedures had been followed, the examiner would have learned only the fact that Peter could not read the word *slice* .

Wixson (1991) refers to the type of instruction that goes on during assessment as "diagnostic teaching." She urges teachers to try several types of alterations, and "to observe the ways in which different reader and contextual factors may be influencing a student's reading" (p. 420). Alterations that teachers might consider include the instructional setting (e.g., from lecture to discussion); the methods of instruction (e.g., from an emphasis on isolated skills to an emphasis on application of skills in authentic reading materials); the materials being used with the student; and the tasks that the student is being asked to perform (e.g., changing from recognition tasks to discussion or open-ended tasks) (p. 240). This approach reflects the philosophy that underlies dynamic assessment, since helping students learn is of primary importance.

While dynamic assessment reflects a change in both the form and function of assessment, there are a number of reform initiatives at the present time that focus mainly on changing the form of assessment. For example, Wixson, *et al.* (1987) report on efforts to develop new statewide tests of reading in Michigan. Advocates of these revised tests claim that they are "based on an interactive view of reading derived from current research and theory" and share "the common goal of reconceptualising reading instruction and assessment within the entire state" (p. 749). In other states, efforts to add a portfolio component to standardized assessment are receiving support (e.g. Vermont's portfolio assessment, Allen, 1991). While these reform efforts might be helpful, they are not in themselves enough to change the ultimate context or function of assessment. "In other words, while these efforts have certainly changed the surface structure of reading assessment, they have not interrogated, much less changed, the assumptions underlying these surface changes" (Bintz & Harste, 1991, p. 233).

Swords to ploughshares

Changing the form and function of literacy assessment might be a more challenging job, but it is necessary if assessment is to become accountable to learning rather than learning accountable to assessment. Instead of seeing assessment as a sword for controlling students, we might consider it as a ploughshare, a tool for helping students learn. This type of assessment will not be as tidy as commercial standardized tests, but as Bintz & Harste (1991) suggest, the time has come to allow ourselves to "get messy with assessment . . . Learning is certainly messy business. Why should assessment be any different?" (pp. 234-235). Assessment will indeed become messy when we cannot distinguish it from instruction. Initially it will seem strange when there are no boundaries to tell us that the learning phase has ended and the testing phase has begun. What will be happening, however, is that our students will continue to learn while being assessed. And what we as educators will derive from this form of assessment is not a set of numerical scores, but knowledge of how our students learn.

References

ALLEN, D. (November, 1991). Vermont's portfolio assessment goes statewide. *The Council Chronicle*, 4.

BINTZ, W., & HARSTE, J. (1991). Whole language assessment and evaluation: The future. In B. Harp (Ed.), *Assessment and evaluation in whole language programs* (pp. 219-242). Norwood, MA: Christopher-Gordon Publishers.

BROZO, W. (1990). Learning how at-risk readers learn best: A case for interactive assessment. *Journal of Reading*, 33(7), 522-527.

CALFEE, R., & HIEBERT, E. (1991). Classroom assessment of reading. In R. Barr, M. Kamil, P. Mosenthal, & P.D. Pearson (Eds.), *Handbook of Reading Research: Vol. 2* (pp. 281-319). New York: Longman.

CAMPIONE, J.C., & BROWN, A.L. (1987). Linking dynamic assessment with school achievement. In C. S. Lidz (Ed.), *Dynamic assessment* (pp. 82 -115). New York: Guilford Press.

CIOFFI, G., & CARNEY, J. (1983). Dynamic assessment of reading disabilities. *The Reading Teacher*, 36, 764-768.

CLAY, M. (1990). Research currents: What is and what might be in evaluation. *Language Arts*, 67(3), 288-298.

FEUERSTEIN, R. (1980). *Instrumental Enrichment: An intervention program for cognitive modifiability*. Baltimore, MD: University Park Press

GOODMAN, K. (1991). An open letter to President Bush. *Whole Language Umbrella Newsletter*.

JOHNSTON, P. (1987). Teachers as evaluation experts. *The Reading Teacher*, 40(8), 744-748.

LIDZ, C.S. (Ed.). (1987). *Dynamic assessment*. New York: Guilford Press.

McCARTHEY, S., & RAPHAEL, T. (1992). Alternative research perspectives. In J. W. Irwin & M.A. Doyle (Eds.), *Reading/writing connections: Learning from research* (pp. 2-30). Newark, DE: International Reading Association.

PARIS, S., LAWTON, T., TURNER, J., & ROTH, J. (1991). A developmental perspective on standardized achievement testing. *Educational Researcher*, 20(5), 12-20.

SATTERLY, D. (1989). *Assessment in schools*. New York: Basil Blackwell Inc.

VYGOTSKY, L. (1962). *Thought and language*. Cambridge, MA: M.I.T. Press.

VYGOTSKY, L. (1978). *Mind in society*. Cambridge, MA: Harvard University Press.

WIXSON, K., PETERS, C., WEBER, E., & ROEBER, E. (1987). New directions in statewide reading assessment. *The Reading Teacher*, 40(8), 749-754.

Teacher Assessment and Literacy at Key Stage 2

Louise Poulson

Assessment has become one of the key issues in British education in the 1990s, largely as a consequence of National Curriculum legislation. Indeed, discussion of the school curriculum without reference to it has become rare and clichés about the relationship between teaching, learning and assessment have become established as self-evident truths (Desforges 1992). Yet, as Desforges argues, there is little, if any, empirical evidence to illuminate the part that assessment might play in teaching and learning.

Research on assessment has however, highlighted both the difficulty and educational undesirability of conflating formative/diagnostic and summative/ evaluative functions (Goldstein, 1990; Goldstein & Noss, 1991, & 1992). These divisions may be illustrated more clearly as being between the private and public dimensions of assessment. The conflation of widely differing functions of assessment within the U.K. National Curriculum model has made conflicting and often incompatible demands on schools. Teachers have been faced with the need to develop effective strategies for giving continuous, formative feedback to pupils and parents and, at the same time, to assess children in order to produce quantitative results for publication. Traditionally, teachers in Primary schools have not been required to undertake formal assessment of children; nor have many Primary school teachers regarded assessment as a part of their professional role (Broadfoot et al. 1991). It is unsurprising, therefore, that teachers in the Primary phase have expressed anxiety about meeting the National Curriculum assessment requirements and have found this to be a stressful process (Broadfoot et al, 1991).

Public awareness of the assessment of literacy is often manifested in concern that standards may be falling; a concern which is not limited to any particular moment in history. Indeed, it seems to have recurred with some regularity since the middle decades of the nineteenth-century. However, evidence from reasonably reliable sources, such as HMI surveys, indicates that there has not been a significant decline in UK literacy standards in recent years. A problem in assessing the extent of literacy within a society at any given time is that a common source of data is the results from standardized tests of reading ability. The use of such data to give information about the extent and degree of literacy is based upon the premise that a more literate school population will be indicated by higher standardized test scores. This is, however, a fallacy. Standardized tests of reading ability show only a very limited range of competence in literacy (Dombey, 1991). First of all, they are concerned only with reading ability and, secondly, they are concerned with the ability to read a limited range of text types in an artificial context. In examining the standardized tests of reading ability used by LEAs, the NFER found that none of them assessed how competent readers actually read in real life (NFER, 1991). Nevertheless, the media debate on reading standards has rested entirely upon the premise that standardized tests indicate the extent of literacy within a population.

Whilst there has been some questioning of what standardized tests actually show as opposed to what it is claimed they show, there has been little analysis of what is to be fully literate in the closing decade of the twentieth-century. Nor have we devised the means by which a more complex version of competence in literacy might be assessed.

The establishment of a statutory National Curriculum and associated assessment procedures might have gone some way towards clarification of these problems. Unfortunately, this seems not to have been the case: more problems have been generated than have been solved.

The Study

It was the aim of a recent research study conducted at the University of Exeter School of Education to examine practices in the teaching and learning of literacy at Key Stage 2. An aspect of this work was concerned with the process of assessing literacy. We wanted to establish what teachers actually did in the classroom context, interacting with pupils and, furthermore, when and how assessment occurred in the classroom. Our concern was to identify the integrated aspects of formative/diagnostic assessment of reading and writing in the Key Stage 2 classroom. A particular difficulty in researching teacher assessment was that much of the advice given by the Schools' Examination and Assessment Council tended to suggest that it was something done apart from on-going classroom activity. Whilst there seemed to be many recommendations as to what teachers should do, there were relatively few accounts of what they actually do in order to gain knowledge of pupil abilities and achievements, or even of how they gained information to inform future teaching decisions. We were concerned to find out not so much how teachers record or report achievement, but how they assess and provide feedback to pupils on work in progress. It seemed that this aspect of the assessment process had been overlooked and yet it was, potentially, the point at which assessment connected most closely with teaching and learning.

In concentrating on teachers of Key Stage 2 children, it was felt that although there was probably an increased awareness of assessment because of the National Curriculum legislation, there was not, at the time, the immediate pressure, as with Key Stage 1 teachers, to fulfil the formal assessment requirements in order to report results. Furthermore, it was felt that if Key Stage 2 teachers were not subject to the immediate pressures of reporting, then they might be more inclined to develop practicable teacher assessment strategies in their classrooms.

We worked in three Primary schools, diverse in location, size and social composition, but all within the same LEA. In each school, we observed part of a normal day's work with a class engaged upon literacy activities and then the same teachers working closely with individual or small groups of children. Finally, the teachers were interviewed about their attitudes to and practices in assessment and the ways in which these had changed since the inception of the National Curriculum. The findings reported here aim only to give an impression, albeit a limited one, of what teachers are doing in terms of giving formative/diagnostic feedback on literacy at Key Stage 2.

Teachers' feelings about National Curriculum assessment

It was clear that all the teachers felt apprehension and had reservations about implementing National Curriculum assessment but in the schools in this study there is evidence that schools and teachers were trying hard to make sense of the requirements. There was a strong feeling that although many adaptations were being made as a result of legislation, they had to be made within the context of the school's ethos. Each school emphasized this point. It was equally clear, as the following comments show, that policy changes could not be made, or implemented, immediately. All the teachers in the study identified similar areas in which they felt that the policy and practice of assessment had changed or was changing as a consequence of the National Curriculum requirements. These can be classified under the following heading: professional development and support; recording and planning; children's awareness and perceptions of assessment.

Professional Development and Support

A coordinated and systematic programme of in-service training and professional development for teachers would seem to be an obvious priority in the successful implementation of the National Curriculum and related assessment practices. However, there is evidence to suggest that this has not been the case. (Poulson & Merchant, 1991; Gill, 1991). The lack of coherent and systematic in-service provision and professional development, on either a national or regional basis, has lead to differences of approach and in the level of support offered by Local Education Authorities. Devolved budgeting and Local Management of Schools in many areas of the country has left many schools and teachers isolated. There is evidence to suggest, in this study and elsewhere, (Poulson & Merchant, 1991) that the most valuable aspects of in-service training for the National Curriculum have been: (i) the opportunity to spend time away form the classroom; (ii) the chance to exchange ideas and discuss practice with colleagues from other schools, HE institutions and the advisory service.

Attitudes to the support provided by the LEA in connection with assessment were varied. Some of the teachers found courses helpful, particularly in providing a starting point for developing strategies and policy within the school. In one instance, a teacher found a course on records of achievement, assessment and reporting for Secondary teachers useful. However, she stressed that in many instances: "the most valuable thing from courses is not the content so much as the support from other people." In some instances teachers were critical of LEA provision which they regarded as being mediocre. It was clear that there had been little time and few opportunities for reflection, or for the development of innovative practices. Where such things had happened, they tended to be developments already initiated, either by LEAs or by schools themselves.

Recording and Planning

There is no doubt that the assessment requirements of the National Curriculum have forced schools to think critically about the planning and recording of work. It was felt to be important that teachers and schools devised means of planning and forms of recording which were inter-related and, furthermore, made sense to themselves, other teachers and even parents. All the teachers stated that planning had become more systematic and that the relationship between planning and recording had become much clearer. However, it was emphasized that that these developments had made demands upon the time and energy of teachers. Whilst it might have seemed more expedient to adopt ready-made systems of recording, particularly in the form of grids or tick sheets, all the teachers maintained that such systems had not worked, in that they had not generated meaningful information about children. They commented in particular on the pointlessness of filling in endless forms.

Diverse ways of planning were identified in relation to the inclusion of National Curriculum Programmes of Study and Attainment Targets. In some cases, planning was done by teachers using the National Curriculum to identify what should be taught and then constructing a programme of work, or topic for a term. Running records in some form were used by all the teachers in order to provide information for the formal written record and report to parents and also to provide indications for future teaching. In the development of systems of recording, the influence of the Primary Language (now Learning) Record was widespread (ILEA/CLPE, 1988). All the teachers in the study were using at least parts of the Record and one used it in its original form. Significant features of the Primary Learning Record, originally developed by the ILEA, include: (i) a research and development period in which materials were trialled and teachers consulted; (ii) a handbook which explains the recording of children's achievement, not only in terms of daily classroom practice, but also within the framework of a theory of learning; (iii) the inclusion of achievement in languages other than English, for bilingual children, where appropriate; (iv) conferences with both parents and children.

Whilst the Primary Language/Learning Record has been influential in the development of systems of recording, it has frequently been modified in various ways. This would seem to suggest that it has been adapted to meet diverse local needs, but also, less positively, that it has been pruned in order to be used without the development and trialling period characteristic of the original. One of the teachers, who had been on the ILEA Primary Language Record working party, was particularly critical of this tendency, viewing it as a short-cut in the development of a recording and reporting system within the LEA.

Identifying Formative Assessment in Key Stage Two Classrooms

The classroom observation of interactions between teachers and pupils revealed a pattern common to all three schools: the assessments which took place were not distinct in procedure from other forms of interaction between teacher and pupils in the classroom. The critical factor in distinguishing an interaction as assessment was that it provided feedback and comment on work completed or in progress. In providing such feedback, the teacher held, in his/her head, a complex and detailed pattern of information about children's achievements and difficulties in literacy. Indeed, teachers in the study reported that the effects of the National Curriculum were both positive and negative in this respect. On the one hand, there was a fear that teachers' judgements would not count unless they were formalised by being written down. But also, as a consequence of having to be more explicit about what was being assessed and in having to find evidence to support their judgements, teachers felt that they had become more reflective about their own practices. They also reported making fewer assumptions about children's achievements and considering with more care what counted as evidence of progress in learning.

The teachers in this study used continuous records, frequently in the form of notebooks, in which events regarded as significant might be written. Significant events were defined by the teachers as: (i) those which indicated that a pupil recognised a problem, or was thinking in a different way about something which had previously caused difficulty; (ii) those which showed pupils beginning to overcome difficulties which previously would have lead them to abandon a task or approach; (iii) those which showed that a pupil was able to approach and complete a task independently where once he/she had needed substantial help; (iv) those which showed that a pupil could complete a task easily where once he/she had struggled.

All the teachers identified the importance of information and evidence about children which he/she held in his/her own head. The impossibility of writing down all observations of events identified as significant by teachers was pointed out. Nevertheless, the teachers in this study felt a covert pressure to make a written record of as much as possible, in that such written records would provide proof of professional judgements made in the classroom. It was clear from classroom observation that teachers' judgements and interventions were embedded within a framework of contextual knowledge. This framework included knowledge of the history of a particular event judged as significant, and its relationship to other events in the classroom. However, as Donaldson (1978) has pointed out, in relation to children's thinking, knowledge embedded within a specific context may be both fragile and, ultimately, limiting. The challenge with which teachers are faced is the disembedding of knowledge of children and their achievements from a specific context and its communication to others.

Pupil's Perceptions of Assessment

If one of the most important purposes of assessment is to give feedback on pupils' progress and to enable teachers to make informed decisions abut what they teach, then it would seem important for the pupils being assessed to be aware of and involved in the process. The schools had developed ways of actively involving pupils in assessment. In one case, pupils made comments on their achievement and progress at the end of a topic project, alongside teachers' comments and those of parents. In another school, using the Primary Learning Record, an agreed comment was made by the teacher and parents in conference and, at a later stage, an agreed comment made by pupil and teacher in conference. Each school involving pupils in assessment stated that it had changed its practice in this respect. In some cases partly as a consequence of National Curriculum requirements, but in no case was it stated as being a direct consequence.

It was recognized that the involvement of pupils in assessment had not happened quickly or easily and, in some cases, they had been initially rather suspicious of being asked to make comments on their own achievement and progress. One teacher commented that at first her class were "very wary" because there was no previous history of them being involved. It was clear that once pupils became involved in assessment, they got better at making critical comments on their own work and performance and became better able to identify their own learning needs. Children also became less competitive about marks and grades given to work and were able to use each other to give feedback and make informal assessments.

During classroom observation, pupils reported that interactions with the teacher had been useful and had helped with their writing or reading. Several emphasized that the teacher was the best person to comment on their work. Whilst peers or paired partners were regarded as useful for discussing books or ideas for writing, pupils were afraid that their peers lacked the teacher's expertise.

However, many commented on the usefulness of peer-feedback in the initial stages of structuring the plot of a story. We were aware, in soliciting pupils' comments on the value of interactions with the teacher, that there might be some distortion: pupils might tell us what they believed we wished to hear. Or, equally, that we might convey comments back to the teacher. The form of questions, therefore, did not require direct comparisons to be made. In many instances, the teachers' interventions served to help children to focus more closely on their task and, if necessary, to reorientate them to its demands.

Some children were more sceptical about the value of interactions with the teacher, as the following comments reveal:

"Asking what I'm going to do doesn't alter what I'm going to do".
"I've learnt how to spell 'learnt', that's all really".
"You feel relieved when she says 'good, fine, good boy'... it means I don't have to write it out again".

In all three schools, observations showed examples of teachers giving feedback to children - an aspect of formative assessment - which were not separate in procedure from the rest of the teaching and which were not planned beforehand. In each case, interactions which could be categorized as assessment were most successful where the teachers' assessment system was in accord with their teaching aims: in short, where teachers gave comments and feedback on the features of writing or reading which the pupils had been actually asked to focus upon in the task. Desforges (1992), and Bennett, Desforges et al. (1984) have documented examples of where the rules for assessment and the feedback given to children are not in accord with what is overtly demanded when a task is set. As they show, where there is such a mismatch, pupils quickly learn the covert rules and consciously aim to meet those requirements in their performance in spite of what the teacher might say he/she wished them to do.

"...regardless of the teachers' expressed aims...(the children) were clear about what would please their teachers. (Bennett, Desforges et al. 1984. 102)

The findings of the study reported here accord with those of Bennett & Desforges, although we generally found a positive correlation between the teachers' stated aims in task-setting and the assessment system which was actually operated in the classroom. Whilst all the teachers maintained that assessment was an ongoing feature of their classrooms, they were not necessarily confident in identifying specific examples out of context. In many instances, the teachers in this study did not immediately identify an interaction as being a part of the assessment process. It was only on reflection, in explaining reasons for actions, that they recognised them as such. This implies that teachers may need to gain confidence in identifying their own assessment system and strategies as well as adopting externally-devised models.

Teachers' Assessment and Evaluation of Pupils' Progress on a One-to-One Basis.

The observation of teacher and pupil interactions in a classroom setting provided an overview of the teacher assessment system in operation during a normal day's activity. In addition, the study aimed also to examine planned and sustained examples of the particular form and content of the assessments to be observed. Interestingly, all chose a form of conferencing with children. In one school, this was an established part of assessment procedure and the Primary Language Record (ILEA/CLPE 1988) was used in an unmodified form. In another, conferencing with children was practised by the teacher who took part in this study, but not necessarily by other teachers in the school. In the third, the class teacher was developing a version of the teacher-pupil conference, although she admitted that it was a relatively new practice to her. The topic of the conferences covered both finished and draft pieces of writing and also reading.

The conference on reading was for the purpose of gaining information and an agreed teacher-pupil comment for the Primary Language Record. The teacher lead the individual children into talking about their recent experiences of reading and asked them to reflect upon these. Questions covered such areas as:
• choice of books being read at the time,
• what the book was about; what had happened in the plot so far (if a narrative),
• evaluation of beginnings and endings of stories,
• comparisons with other books/authors,
• ways of reading: individual/partnerships with other children,
• when reading is done: home/school; specific times/places,
• relationship between reading and writing (and other forms of representation): how reading influenced pupils' own writing; getting ideas from other writers; ways of telling and structuring a narrative,
• reflection upon pupils' own achievement in literacy and areas for further development.

It can be seen from the range of topics covered that the discussion between teacher and pupils was searching. It emerged very clearly that the children were able to articulate their practices in reading and to identify aspects of the relationship between reading and writing. This was not only with reference to a small sample of reading matter, but across a wide range of texts and genres. The teacher was enabled an insight into the social practices of reading in her classroom and factors influencing the pattern of reading.

Children most frequently referred to the visual/graphic dimensions of a book as being the most influential in their choice of a text by an unknown author. Furthermore, their appraisal of the graphic aspects of texts was not superficial: sophisticated observations were made of the relationship between the written and visual text. Connections were made between the children's own writing and the books which they had read with a conscious focus upon the constructedness of written text. Familiarity with intertextual reference was shown in drawing upon their own and other children's experience of texts to inform understanding of the ways in which books work. They made comparisons between ways in which stories were narrated by different authors, drawing distinctions between the order of events and the ways in which these are disclosed - Genette's (1980) concepts of *histoire* and *récit*. This has already been identified in relation to younger children's understanding of narrative structure (Poulson 1991), but in the instances of older children outlined in this study, there was an explicitly articulated understanding. There was, in fact, a network of information in this particular class about books and reading; which of the children's own books were being circulated; who had read which books; which were the currently popular texts; where to go to for advice on choice of book; whose recommendation and opinions counted.

The teacher-pupil conferences on children's writing generated evidence of an equally sophisticated awareness of text construction: one in which the two dimensions of writing identified as secretarial and compositional in the National Curriculum English document (DES, 1989) were interwoven. The National Curriculum for English allocates a much greater weighting to the compositional aspects of writing, but much research evidence (e.g. Britton et al. 1976; Kress 1982; Bennett, Desforges et al. 1984) has revealed the limited extent to which children are taught, and presumably, assessed in this aspect of writing. Most attention tends to be paid to the surface, orthographic features of children's writing, in spite of the rhetoric about current practice. In observing teacher-pupil conferences, we found examples of both aspects being interwoven in written text construction.

The assessments made by the teacher in this instance included the contribution that orthographic features of writing made to the composition of a text. For example, how the inclusion of commas to mark off main and subordinate clauses would contribute to overall coherence. Additionally, how the use of quotation marks and other conventions for distinguishing between direct speech and reportage actually signalled and marked out category boundaries and discourse shifts within a text. In one instance, the teacher showed the child an example of this from a familiar book, requiring the pupil to shift her perspective from that of writer to that of reader of her own text.

The need for cohesive devices within written text and how inconsistency, or a lack of cohesive signalling might make reading difficult, was explained in several of the writing conferences. One such example was in the use of the conjunction 'but', normally used to indicate contrast or concession between propositions, but in this case used to indicate a relationship of reason-result and, therefore, the relationship of concession between two propositions was unclear. When this was pointed out, the pupil remarked that: "...the 'but' takes it back... in the story."

The instances described above indicate that the teachers were concerned with more than the ability to decode print, or to construct near and correctly spelled examples of written text. Each, in different ways, was attempting to encourage children to solve problems in literacy. They were not only concerned with the child's mastery of particular aspects of reading or writing, but also with the identification of patterns and relationships within written texts. Thus, evidence of achievement of progress might include mastery of a particular aspect of reading or writing, or equally, might be the beginning of a child's recognition of the necessity of particular features of text organisation in the construction of meaning.

It is clear that the teachers in this study made judgements about and provided feed back on a wide range of literacy events. Even so, these interactions may not have been viewed explicitly as assessment. No pre-devised assessment instrument was used, but evidence of pupil achievement was being gathered. Not only was evidence being gathered of pupil achievement at a particular moment in time, but also the teachers were often aware of what pupils might achieve in the future.

Conclusion.

We had started the research with an implicit hypothesis: that specific examples of assessment by teachers would be detectable from observation. The hypothesis was only partly supported and further questions were raised. These included: how these particular instances of teachers' practice in providing feedback to children on literacy events might be recognised more clearly, by the teachers themselves, as contributing to formative assessment. Equally, how teachers might be encouraged to identify and articulate their own, often implicit, assessment systems and to relate these to other less individual and idiosyncratic models of assessment. Furthermore, the question was raised of how the evidence of children's achievement generated in the classroom might be validated and, where necessary be made reliable. Desforges (1992) suggests that the key question in establishing the validity of assessment is the extent to which a particular procedure or system promotes quality learning. It is a critical question, but one which is seldom asked when the focus of assessment becomes the reliability of results found in large samples of children engaged in a limited range of literacy events.

For literacy to be understood as a complex activity, then it is necessary to understand the range of literate practices with which children are familiar. It is clearly not enough to focus upon the teaching and learning of grapho-phonemic or, for that matter, grapho-morphemic features of written text nor upon the syntactic structure of small segments of text. This is not the sum total of literacy, nor should it be represented as such, but there is, however, a danger of it coming to be the sum total of literacy assessed. In identifying, if not defining, quality learning in literacy, it is necessary to return to the importance of representing not a narrow conception of literate competence, but one appropriate to the complex demands of the late twentieth-century. One which fully acknowledges the cognitive demands of reading and writing as inter-related dimensions of the same cultural process.

References

BARRS, M., ELLIS S AND THOMAS, A. (1988) *The Primary Language Record.* London: ILEA/CLPE

BENNETT, N., DESFORGES, C et al. (1984) *The Quality of Pupil Learning Experiences* London: Lawrence Erlbaum Associates.

BRITTON, J. et al (1975) *The Development of Writing Abilities 11-18* :London: Macmillan.

BROADFOOT, P. et al. (1991) 'Implementing National Assessment: issues for Primary teachers' in *Cambridge Journal of Education* Vol. 21 No.2

DESFORGES, C. (1992) 'Assessment and Learning' in *Forum* Vol 34. No. 4.

DOMBEY, H. (1991) 'Testing Times for Infant Reading'. in WRAY, D (Ed) *Standards in Reading. (Perspectives 44.)* Exeter: University of Exeter School of Education.

DONALDSON, M. (1978) *Children's Minds* London: Fontana

GENETTE, J. (1980) *Narrative Discourse* (trans. Lewin, J.) Oxford: Blackwell.

GILL, P. (1991) 'INSET in the introduction of the National Curriculum: A Critical View' in *British Journal of In-Service Education*. Vol.17 No.1

GOLDSTEIN, H. (1990) *National Curriculum Assessment*. Lecture given to Language in Inner City Schools Conference, June 1990. London University Institute of Education.

GOLDSTEIN, H. AND NOSS, R. (1991) 'Against the Stream' in *Forum* Vol. 33 No.1

KRESS, G. (1982) *Learning to Write* London: Routledge & Kegan Paul.

N.F.E.R. (1991) *An Inquiry into LEA Evidence on Standards of Reading of Seven-Year Old Children* London: NFER

NOSS, R. AND GOLDSTEIN, H. (1992) 'Alternative Currents' in *Forum* Vol. 34. No.1

POULSON, L. (1991) 'Narrative in the Infant Classroom' in *English in Education*. Vol 25. No.1

POULSON, L. & MERCHANT, G. (1991) 'National Curriculum Training and Teachers' Professional Development' in *British Journal of In-Service Education*. Vol. 17. No.1.

Family Literacy in Australia

Julie Spreadbury

The Project

This study examines the complex three-way interactions that take place when a parent and a child share a text. It endeavours to tease out the particular factors in this interaction that facilitate the child's later reading ability. As part of this, the study also investigates parent styles in such book reading episodes and how these change from when the child is a dependent reader to when the child is an independent reader, i.e. the transition period from the end of the child's Preschool Year to the end of the first year in Primary School. This period appears to have been neglected by researchers in early literacy.

Over the past 40 years, research has focussed increasingly on the home as the main factor in children's language development. In the last ten years in particular, parent and child book reading episodes in the home have been foregrounded as a major factor in children's literacy development. But in spite of the research that has been carried out, much is still unknown about what factors bring about this literacy growth, in particular the possible role of parent-child storybook-reading.

A parent reading a book to a child in the home is an important part of the cultural tradition of many Australians. When a parent reads with a child literacy learning occurs. Research has been carried out on the texts for young children (e.g. Meek, 1988; Williams, 1989) and on the verbal interaction between mother and child (e.g. Snow, 1977, 1983; Tizard and Hughes, 1984; Wells, 1986) but the triple interactions that take place when a parent and a child share a book together have been neglected. Martinez and Roser (1985) point out that these studies are needed so that *"we begin to have a clearer notion of the adult-child-text relationship during story time. Such an understanding may eventually provide adults working with young children with a basis for determining how best to guide children toward successfully interacting with texts. However additional research is needed before specific recommendations can be made...studies with other books, other adult-child dyads, and with additional text factors may aid in better understanding the language behaviour of children and adults during story time"* (p. 293)

The present study was born out of curiosity to know more about what parents do when they read with their child in the home, especially in this transition period from the end of Preschool to the end of Year 1. The data have been drawn from many different sources - from the children, parents, siblings and teachers concerned using interviews, observations, video transcripts, and standardised tests. Different analyses have been used to explore which factors are critical to a child's literacy learning. These factors have been measured against the 'consistent analytical framework' (Teale & Sulzby, 1986, p. 199) that language is learnt through interaction with other people. This means not merely oral language but also literacy. The present study seeks to show that it is the interaction between parent and child that takes place when a parent and child read together that teaches the child to read, not merely reading to the child in a performance-like manner. This is not formal teaching but rather that the child internalises the information contained in such interactions in the home.

Design

A longitudinal study over a twelve month period from the end of the children's Preschool Year to the end of Year 1 at Primary School was conducted. It incorporated an analysis of parent-child book reading episodes in the home with the parents reading an unfamiliar text. The study also involved assessment of the children's language and reading attainments and self concept. Interviews with parents and teachers and observations of teachers' group story reading behaviour were conducted.

Subjects

The subjects were 25 children drawn randomly from the two Year 1 classes at a State Primary School in Brisbane. This school was chosen because it has varied socio-economic levels. 15 were boys and 11 were girls. One of the girls left the study in March of her Year 1 as her family moved to seek employment. At the beginning of Year 1, the majority of the children had turned six (16), nine were five year olds and one child was slightly older at seven. The majority of children (21) had been born in Brisbane while two others had been born in other towns in Queensland. Two children were born in other states of Australia, while one was born in New Zealand. Two subjects were only children, but the majority (14) were the oldest child while three were in the middle, and seven were the youngest child in the family.

All families had a mother who had at least some high school education, though only three had Bachelor's degrees and two had other post-school education. In contrast, in the 23 families with a father, one had no high school education, but more fathers than mothers had post-school qualifications. Fathers' occupations ranged from medical doctor, research scientist and engineer through such occupations as electrician, draughtsman, and technical officer to three fathers being unemployed. On the other hand, the occupations of the mothers who worked outside the home were not as varied with a bank officer being the most prestigious, down through secretarial work and shop assistant to nursing home aide. Apart from the previously mentioned family which transferred interstate, another couple were divorced and one father died suddenly towards the end of first year of the study. There were two house-husbands and three more mothers were working full-time by the end of the first year of the study. These families have remained in the study.

Data collection instruments / procedures

At the end of the child's preschool and at the end of Year 1 at school, I went in to each child's home and interviewed the parent about demographic aspects of the family, the families' literacy practices and parents' attitudes and ideologies about literacy. On both occasions, the parent and child were videoed reading the picture book, *Sloppy Kisses* which was chosen because it had just been published and so was an unknown text to all the families. By videoing all the dyads of parent and child reading the same text there was a basis for comparison. In most homes only one parent read to the child, in others both mother and father read the texts.

I also interviewed the children's teachers at both Preschool and Year 1 and videoed them reading to groups of the children as part of their daily routine but I will report on those findings at a later date.

Results and discussion

Because of limited space only some of the results of the study will be discussed here. During both readings parents showed great variation in individual style of reading *Sloppy Kisses*. It is interesting to note that no parents discussed the cover of the text but a few parents contextualised the narrative by linking it to their child's past experience as Brendan's mother does in this Preschool reading -

Mother: We'll read Sloppy Kisses first. Sloppy Kisses Brendan, that's like the kids don't like me kissing them with my lipstick on, eh?
Brendan: (laughing) Yeah!

During the reading, parents focussed on the story meaning, not on word meaning. Only one parent explained a word meaning to her child - 'papa' for 'daddy' or 'father - a word only used by one family in the study. There was no discussion in either the Preschool or the Year 1 readings of letters or indeed 'print'.

Several parents focussed the discussion on the illustrations in the text as in this Preschool reading by Samantha's mother:

Mother: (Reads) Emmy Lou kissed Papa goodbye when she went to school. And when they came home, it started all over again. Emmy Lou's family just loved to kiss.

Mother: There's Papa going to work. They're a funny family aren't they? They look like piggies.

Sam: They are! (laughs) Oh look at that! (points to illustration)

Mother: Have you ever seen a piggy kiss? I reckon they grunt (makes grunting noise)

Sam: Yes ! (Mother and Sam both laugh)

There are also frequent examples in the transcripts of children modelling questions on those of the parent reading to them, for example, in the Preschool reading of *Sloppy Kisses* after: 'Emmy Lou snuggled down under her covers. It took her a long time to get to sleep', Alice's mother asked, 'I wonder why?', an inferential question that Alice did not answer. Later during the same reading after 'One night Emmy Lou couldn't get to sleep...No matter what she did she could not get to sleep", Alice asked the same question 'I wonder why?' Her mother answered 'I don't know. Let's read on.' During both readings parents asked many inferential questions which their children did not respond to. Alice's mother's 'I wonder why' was asked by 10 parents over both readings and was mostly allowed to 'plop' or be ignored by the child. In some readings where the child was unable to answer the question, the parent 'scaffolded' or helped the child succeed by providing more information as in this interaction with Sean and his mother during the Year 1 reading:

Mother: (Reads) It took her a long time to get to sleep.

Mother: Why do you think it took her so long to get to sleep?

Sean: Cause she was thinking.

Mother: She just had a pat on the shoulder instead of her usual kiss goodnight, didn't she?

Here, Sean's mother provided him with the necessary information in the form of a *confirm-verify-reassure* type question, a tag question which threw the conversation over to him. He responded nonverbally by nodding his head to show he understood.

When a child could not answer an inferential question, some parents provided more information as Sean's mother did, but then dropped the level of comprehension required by asking a determinate comprehension question as in this interaction between Brian and his mother during the Year 1 reading:

Mother: Why do you think it took her a long time to get to sleep? (INFERENTIAL) She's thinking about what they said about kissing. (PROVIDING INFORMATION) You find it easy to get to sleep cause you always have a kiss goodnight, don't you? (DETERMINATE)

In the highly interactive dyads, many parents 'upped the ante' during the Year 1 reading by asking questions that demanded a higher level of comprehension from their child. The parents were apparently unaware of doing this, that is, they were interacting with their child during the reading, not consciously teaching the child. This fits the research findings of Snow, Perlmann & Nathan (1983) that parents use simpler lexis and grammatical structure to converse with a baby than with an older child.

During the readings of *Sloppy Kisses* some parents even focussed their discussion at a deeper level on the ideology of the text. An analysis of the discourse between two dyads during the reading of *Sloppy Kisses* shows that both mothers used similar strategies to transmit the ideology of the text. Both used tag questions i.e. *confirm-verify-probe* or *confirm-verify-reassure* questions to include their child in the conversation while directing attention to the ideology by explicit information providing statements. They also linked the ideology included in the text to their child's own everyday experience thus making it real and powerful for the child.

No parent asked any comprehension questions at the end of the text at either Preschool or Year 1 levels. They did, however, frequently comment on their own enjoyment of the book or ask if the child enjoyed the text.

Although the parents produced more utterances overall than the children, in the highly interactive dyads, the power was shared by parent and child, with the child contributing questions and comments, not merely responding to the parent's questions and comments. This was in contrast to the Year 1 teachers' readings where the teacher alone controlled the interaction.

There appeared to be significant changes in interactions from Preschool to Year 1. The number of parent utterances during the reading of *Sloppy Kisses* decreased from Preschool to Year 1. There was great variation in parent reading style ranging from those who were highly interactive with their child to those who had little or no verbal interaction. The decrease in interaction from Preschool to Year 1 can be seen at the non-interactive end of this continuum where there were three dyads with no interaction at the Preschool level but ten dyads with no interaction and five with only one or two utterances at the Year 1 level. This is in keeping with Heath's (1984) findings that interactive behaviour during story reading episodes in the home changes as the child gets older. Initially, parents seem to encourage interaction but later expect the child to sit still, listen quietly to the text, and gain information from it as they are expected to do in many classrooms.

163

The amount of child comment at the Year 1 reading fell by a highly significant degree which might suggest that even after one year of formal schooling children have learned to be passive listeners of stories, not actively interacting with either the person reading the text nor the text itself. This may be because at Year 1 level these children had been read to as a whole class of twenty children, not individually or in small groups as they had been at Preschool and in the home.

Some correlations

By using standardised reading test scores some interesting correlations were derived. Of greatest significance was the high correlation between the number of parent utterances and children's reading at both six and eight. This suggests that it is not merely reading to the child which facilitates their reading but the amount of interaction between parent and child. The correlation between the child's reading at age six and eight with alternate questions, in particular tag questions, suggests also that it is not merely the amount but also the type of talk which matters. Tag questions, as Snow (1977) suggests, pass the conversation over to the child thus affirming the child and also increasing the interaction. This is also verified by the correlation of parent utterances and the child's self concept and, in turn, the correlation of self concept with reading at both six and eight. Overall, the number and level of correlation between the variables strongly suggest that reading aloud in the home is of great influence on the child's reading ability at school.

Implications

This study has revealed that parent, child and text reading aloud in the home changes in the transition period from Preschool when most children are dependent readers to Year 1, when most are independent readers at least on suitable text. It shows that reading is a social process, learnt in interaction with other people. Family storybook reading is seen as a vital social construct for the child's later independent reading. This has implications which apply to parents, teachers and schools, and society at large.

From the study, parents have shown they facilitate their child's literacy learning long before the child begins formal schooling. Parents do this across all educational and socio-economic levels, instinctively adapting the language they use in interactions with their child to suit the language level, including the reading level, of the child. It is the interaction between parent and child that takes place when a parent reads to a child that facilitates this child's reading. In particular, reading is aided by the types of questions that the parent uses. Some of these questions, commonly known as 'tag questions' or labelled *confirm-verify-probe* and *confirm-verify-reassure*, pass the conversation over to the child. This not only makes the child responsible for his/her own learning but also, and perhaps more importantly, appears to strengthen the relationship between parent and child. *Confirm-enquire-ask* questions, where the verbal process comes first as in 'Did you see the mother?' and *apprize-precise-specify* questions, the 'wh' questions that require specific information, also correlate with the child's reading ability at both age six and eight. A more specific study, with a larger sample, is needed to investigate further which parent question types during book reading sessions help children to read, and exactly how these types of questions facilitate children's reading ability.

A most important implication for parents from the study is that its positive findings need widespread dissemination to parents via the media, school and parent groups. Parents need to be told that they are most important to their children's intellectual growth, not least of all because of the close affective links between parent and child. Future research is required to investigate more fully the importance of these affective links with the child's ability to read.

These findings have implications for parent programmes in particular. Many existing programmes for parents begin with the premise that parents have a great deal to learn from teachers. The findings of this study shake the very foundation of this belief. They suggest that parents of varying socio-economic and educational levels are teaching their children essential literacy concepts and skills during everyday reading aloud sessions in the home.

There is also a glaring need for more longitudinal studies of family literacy practices in low socio-economic families for, although this study shows that socioeconomic levels overall were uncorrelated with the other variables, it may be significant that socio-economic levels did correlate with the children's reading ability at age 8. More in-depth and longitudinal studies of low socio-economic families are needed to understand this correlation more fully. Studies are likewise needed to explore if, indeed, story reading in low socio-economic families is a different literacy event than it is in schools. This study suggests there are some children who, from their family book reading practices, have been familiarised with the same types of questions that teachers use during book reading episodes in school. It may be that these children are advantaged at school, compared with children who have come from family environments where literacy events are quite different from those in the classroom.

Teachers need to see parents as partners in fostering children literacy growth. This has implications for reading pedagogy. The findings of the study that it is the interaction between the adult and child during reading aloud that facilitates children's reading ability, not merely reading aloud to a child, has serious implications for classroom strategies and would seem to suggest that what is called 'paired reading' is a more suitable strategy for Year 1. This would necessitate more adults being actively involved in the classroom, either parents or other community members. Clearly there is a vast, largely untapped resource of competent adult support for children's reading already in existent in the wider community. Research is needed to investigate strategies for maximising the potential of this resource.

References

HEATH, S.B. with THOMAS, C. (1984) The achievements of preschool literacy for mother and child. In Goelman, H., Oberg, A. & Smith, F. (eds.) *Awakening to Literacy*. London: Heinemann.

MARTINEZ, M. & ROSER, N. (1985) Read it again : the value of repeated readings during storytime. *The Reading Teacher*, April, 782-786.

MEEK, M. (1988) *How Texts Teach What Readers Learn*. Stroud: Thimble Press.

PELLIGRINI, A. (1991) Critique of the concept of at risk as applied to emergent literacy. *Language Arts*, 68, 380-385.

SNOW, C. (1977) The development of conversation between mothers and babies. *Journal of Child Language*, 4, 1-22.

SNOW, C. (1983) Literacy and language : relationships during preschool years. *Harvard Education Review*, 53, 165-189.

SNOW, C., PERLMANN, R & NATHAN, D. (1986) Why routines are different: towards a multiple-factors model of the relation between input and language acquisition. In Nelson, K. (Ed.) *Children's Language*. Hillsdale: Lawrence Erlbaum.

TEALE, W.H. & SULZBY, E. (Eds.) (1986) *Emergent Literacy: Writing and Reading*. New Jersey: Ablex.

TIZARD, B. & HUGHES, M. (1984) *Young Children Learning : Talking and Thinking at Home and at School*. London: Fontana.

WELLS, G. (1986) *The Meaning Makers* Portsmouth : Heinemann.

WILLIAMS, G. (1989) Naive and serious questions : the role of text criticism in primary education. In Meek, M. & Mills, C. (Eds.) *Language and Literacy in the Primary School*. London : Falmer Press.

Home as the Primary Context for Young Children's Literacy Development

Jo Weinberger

Several researchers of young children's interactions with print have made clear that literacy learning can begin from a very early age, e.g. Goodman (1980), Teale and Sulzby (1986). That means it begins at home. However, schools often at best underestimate, and at worst, overlook the extent to which all children learn about literacy at home in their early years.

What sort of context does their home provide for young children's literacy development? As a nursery teacher, I suspected that the children joining the nursery unit where I worked had had a variety of literacy experiences at home, but I did not know what sorts of experiences, nor how common they were among the group as a whole. Bearing in mind that what young learners of literacy need is access to reading and writing materials, opportunities to watch what more experienced readers and writers do, and times when reading and writing are a part of everyday activities, I was interested in the answers to three key questions:
1. What access do preschool children have to reading and writing materials?
2. To what extent do parents act as literacy models for their children?
3. What literacy learning is involved in the day-to-day activities of parents and children at home?

Although some previous research has looked at children's early literacy development at home, e.g. Heath (1983), Payton (1984), Teal (1986), Taylor and Dorsey Gaines (1988), Hannon and James (1990), this has provided only partial answers.

An exploratory study

A way to find answers to the questions posed above would be to ask parents themselves. About five years ago, I started to interview parents of children due to start nursery about their children's literacy at home. The average age of children at the time was three and a half.

The area from which the families came comprised a traditional village, a large council estate, and small but growing estates of private housing, situated on the outskirts of a large city. There was a variation in social class amongst the families, (but not of ethnic group and language). 20 of the families were middle class and 40 were working class (using the Registrar General's classifications). All families were white and spoke English as a first language apart from one Chinese family where English was a second language.

Findings of the study

What access do preschool children have to reading and writing materials?

I found that the range of materials varied considerably between families, but reading and writing materials were available in all the homes. The variation occurred within the social class groupings as well as between them.

Books

All children had some access to children's books, and the use of children's books was taken as a matter of course in all but one family. Even in that family, children's books were used. The mother, who herself found reading difficult, had recently bought three books on advice from the local health visitor to share books with her child. (This child also looked through a Sunday colour supplement, so other written material would have been available at home even though her mother had not at first thought of introducing books).

About a quarter of the children borrowed books from the library, often frequently, although the majority (almost three quarters) did not borrow library books at all. The number of children's books available at home varied widely, from none, to the child who owned 200 books at least, and was also a member of the library. Those that owned the least books were also the least likely to borrow them. About a quarter of the children owned less than a dozen books each, and of these only two used the library.

However, it was very rare for the children to own no books at all, and then it was due to exceptional circumstances. In this sample, only two children owned no books at all at the time of interview, and both had recently, and hastily, moved away from difficult domestic situations and had not yet become fully established in their new homes. So, for only a small proportion of the children access to books was very limited.

For most children there was a difference between what they read at home, and what they would later find in school. When parents were asked about the books the children owned, only seven parents mentioned the type of picture books found in nursery. In particular, the children's expectations of narrative deriving from what they encountered at home were different from what they would soon experience in books in the nursery, which could be characterized as literature specifically written for children, and pitched at a developmentally appropriate level. This is not to denigrate the importance of children's encounters with other types of books at home. These give access to the world of print, and to notions of being a reader. It is, however, to emphasise the gulf that exists between what most children read at home, and what they will later be expected to read at school.

As for the books, at least half the parents mentioned those published by Ladybird. The most often mentioned books by title were those about Thomas the Tank Engine. At the time of the interviews, there was a series of that name on television, and the stories and logo were being aggressively marketed. Books about other characters familiar on television were also mentioned e.g. Postman Pat, Mr. Men, Shoe People, He-Man and Thundercats. A few non-fiction books were mentioned; ABC and counting books, books about animals, books about going to the dentist and to hospital, an encyclopedia, picture dictionary and a book of Bible stories. As one might expect, other popular books contained traditional stories and nursery rhymes. The children also looked at and read reading scheme books, comics, bath books, cloth books, colour books, annuals, lift-the-flap books, books with cassettes, and books with videos.

The majority of books owned by the children were selected from those most readily available. This was usually from local shops, often the post office, newsagents, or nearest supermarket. Books were also bought through bookclubs, although several parents commented that these books were rather expensive. Some parents bought books in a 'bookshop' in town (there were none locally). Most frequently, this was the Early Learning Centre, or at W.H. Smith - shops which also sold other goods. Only three of the parents mentioned buying books in bookshops. Some parents may not have known about the many types of books that were available for preschool children, and therefore would not have sought out items they did not know existed. Weinberger (1988) and Hannon, Weinberger and Nutbrown (1991), both referring to similar groups of parents, document parents' surprise at the range of books produced for young children.

For the majority of children, books at home were those most widely distributed and relatively cheap. I suspect they were often bought while shopping as an object, together with, or in place of, a small toy or sweets, with the child often initially attracted by a familiar character or logo on the cover. The type of picture book found in nursery was not encountered so frequently by parents and children when shopping, an observation also made by Toomey and Sloane (in press), and also, these were seen in some cases to be too expensive.

Other printed material

Children are often avid consumers of print, able to make sense of general printed matter, as well as material specifically designed for them. For example, the majority of the children in this sample looked through mail order catalogues, and many read other 'adult' items, for example: magazines, newspapers, dictionaries, Bible and prayer books, and trade magazines. In all, the range of printed materials to which this group of children had access was considerable.

Resources for drawing and writing

Resources for drawing and writing were available to all the children. Although some parents thought their children were too young to 'write', the materials were there if the child had wanted to do so. Activities such as drawing, colouring in, and 'scribbling' were all regarded by the parents as normal everyday activities for the children. Some of the preschool children were extremely well resourced, and some children had very little, but all of them had access to reading and writing materials, and had made a start on using these resources well before their entry to nursery.

To what extent do parents act as literacy models for their children?

When children see others at home reading and writing, they learn 'unconscious' lessons that they can then internalise about what it is to be a reader or writer. For most children, parents are their most significant role models. In this sample parents reported that all children saw them either reading or writing. However, some read and wrote considerably more than others, and some were more conscious of their role a model for their children.

The only parent who said her son did not see her reading to herself was one of a small number of parents who had difficulties with reading. "I don't read for myself. I only read because of the children. I hate reading. There's lots of words I don't know so I skip them. I never read for pleasure." Despite this, she appreciated the importance of helping her children with literacy and how they might copy her behaviour. She did look at books with the children, and commented elsewhere during the interview. "He's got the idea of picking up a book and looking at it. He might have copied off me - seeing me pick up books."

Four parents thought their children saw them read regularly, but did not see them write. Apart from these exceptions, other parents were able to provide numerous examples of the reading and writing they were doing at home, which their children might observe. Many of the parents felt the pressure of time in looking after young children, and said they did not read for pleasure, often adding that they used to.

However, reading was still a well-established part of most families' daily routine, and children had regular opportunities to see their parents read for directly practical purposes and to find out information. Examples, observed by their children, included parents reading: newspapers, magazines read by both women and men, books, catalogues, knitting and crochet patterns, TV guides, puzzle books, professional journals and papers, teletext and their mail.

The parents also generated a long list of writing they did at home. This included: writing shopping lists, bank statements, directions, crosswords, keeping a diary, appointments, notes, cheques, bills, letters, writing for work, word processing, running clubs, filling in forms and coupons, party invitations, writing for study, sending for mail order items, keeping books, word searches, invoices, letters, Spot the Ball and Pools coupons, DSS forms, cards, accounts, bank paying in slips, desktop publishing, and writing to do with being a school governor. Some parents did only one or two of the activities listed above. Others did many, and read and wrote extensively at home.

For several children, the experience of seeing a parent read or write appeared to have prompted the child to imitate their behaviour.

"I think his interest in reading comes from me, probably because he sees me read a lot".
"He gets out the Autotrader. What sets him off is my husband looking through the Autotrader".
"She likes to watch me write a shopping list and then she 'writes' hers".

Some parents were aware of the impact of these experiences, and deliberately encouraged their children to participate too.

"If I'm reading a book, I'll ask him to sit and 'read' with me, and he does".
"I sell Avon now. We have a game at doing Avon. I get all the little forms out and she thinks she's helping. She loves that".
"I type my husband's work invoices. It's ended up with buying him a typewriter because he wanted to join in".

There was variation in the extent to which parents provided a model, along a continuum from minimal to extensive uses of literacy, but among this sample all the parents at some time provided a role model in the uses of literacy for their children.

What literacy learning is involved in the day-to-day activities of parents and children at home?

The majority of parents said that they were specifically teaching their preschool children to read, write, or to interpret environmental print. A few parents persevered in trying to teach reading or writing, even thought they felt they were battling against their child's lack of maturity and interest. But most parents were sensitive to the developmental stage their child had reached and adjusted their input accordingly. They used a variety of both formal and informal methods.

A few parents mentioned that they had bought ready made resources to help them teach their child to learn to read and write. This type of resource is becoming increasingly prominent, and the pressure on parents to buy them has increased with the advent of the National Curriculum, and scares about reading failure. However, in this sample, they were not widely used, and often those parents who had tried them commented that their children were still too young for them. Similar comments were made about much of the more 'formal' teaching of literacy that they tried with their children.

Parents were asked to name resources and activities helpful for children's literacy development that their children made use of, or took part in. By their replies, parents demonstrated a broad interpretation of what was useful for literacy.

One of the strengths of the home is that it offers children the chance of uncontrived learning situations. Much occurs naturally, without parents consciously noticing that it is helpful for literacy, as Leichter (1974) comments, the transmission of literacy often "occurs at the margins of awareness". Nevertheless, unprompted, the list of what the parents themselves picked out as being helpful to their children's literacy development was substantial, wide ranging, and often embedded in day-to-day family activities. The illustrations given in Table 1 combine to give a flavour of the sorts of things that were happening at home.

Table 1
Activities encouraging children's literacy development at home

- writing and drawing in steam on the windows
- selecting shopping by the label
- writing a shopping list
- writing names in cards
- child writing their name on drawings
- reading and writing alongside their parent
- reading letters to the child

- playing at libraries
- playing games with matching, listening and sorting activities
- using games incorporating the alphabet
- doing jigsaws
- cutting and sticking using old catalogues
- playing at school
- watching television together
- child watching television programmes
- reading things off the television
- following up ideas from children's television programmes
- recognising product labels
- baking
- modelling with plasticine and playdough
- taking the child out
- saying and singing nursery rhymes
- listening to cassettes with songs
- operating washing machine
- using a home computer
- filling in bank paying-in slips
- putting laundry away
- looking at pictures
- looking at photo albums

The difference between families was again evident, with some parents involving their children in many activities, and others doing only a little. But it is worth pointing out that something was going on in all the homes.

The pressure to standardise what is available at home is starting to come through the National Curriculum, the media, and the proliferation of products designed to help parents 'teach' their children. It would be a loss if what is already happening is not acknowledged and built upon.

Conclusion

There was a wide variety of literacy on offer to children in the study, in terms of quantity and appropriateness, including the style of presentation, from the naturalistic to the more formal.

Some children had many resources for literacy, and others had very few. The type and extent varied considerably. But all children had some access to books and others printed matter, and to paper and writing implements. There was variation within social class groupings as well as between them. All parents read or wrote in front of their children. Some parents were aware of their role as models, and some also built on this as a way of encouraging their child to read and write. The majority of parents deliberately taught their child about literacy. However, much meaningful literacy learning was embedded within the ordinary everyday activities of parents and their preschool children. In all the families in this sample, children had learnt some understanding about literacy and had developed some literacy skills, before they started at nursery.

The research reported here is part of a longitudinal study. This will allow explorations of features of the young child's early home context which are related to literacy attainments later.

References

GOODMAN, Y. (1980) The roots of literacy. *Claremont Reading Conference Yearbook*, 44, 1-12.

HANNON, P., & JAMES, S. (1990) Parents' and teachers' perspectives on preschool literacy development. *British Educational Research Journal*, 16, 3, 259-272.

HANNON, P. WEINBERGER, J., & NUTBROWN, C. (1991) A study of work with parents to promote early literacy development. *Research Papers in Education*, 6, 2, 77-97.

HEATH, S.B. (1983) *Ways with words: language, life and work in communities and classrooms*. Cambridge: Cambridge University Press.

LEICHTER, H.J. (1974) The family as educator. *Teachers College Record*, 76, 175-217.

PAYTON, S. (1984) *Developing awareness of print*. Educational Review, occasional publications No.2. Birmingham: University of Birmingham.

TAYLOR, D. AND DORSEY-GAINES, C. (1988) *Growing up literate: learning from inner city families*. Portsmouth, N.H. : Heinemann.

TEALE, W.H., (1986) Home background and young children's literacy development. In W.H.Teale and E.Sulzby (eds) *Emergent literacy: writing and reading*. Norwood, N.J.: Ablex.

TEALE, W.H. & SULZBY, E. (eds) (1986) *Emergent literacy: writing and reading*. Norwood,N.J.: Ablex.

TOOMEY, D., & SLOANE, J. (in press) Fostering children's early literacy development through parent involvement: a five year program. In D. Dickson (ed) *Bridges for literacy: approaches to supporting child and family literacy*. Oxford: Blackwell.

WEINBERGER, J. (1988) Reading: parents and preschool. *Reading*, 22, 3, 164-167.

Readers meet Texts: LINC and the Teaching of Reading

Margaret Cook and Sylvia Karavis

Within England and Wales, "LINC" has become associated with anti-traditional and anti-governmental approaches to language education while in some respects appearing also to threaten what might broadly be termed the "apprenticeship" approach to language development. Outside its geo-political context, LINC may well appear as a small though interesting event in the history of twentieth century language education, relating, however tangentially, to the influences of writers and educators such as Smith and Harste in the USA, Halliday and Kress in Australia and a range of British educators from the authors of *Language in Use* and the Bullock Report to Britten, Barnes and, more recently, the *National Writing Project* team.

When the dust settles it may well be that LINC's place in this history relates more to what the programme's training pack attempted than what it achieved. What is unique to the LINC materials is their endeavour (not always successful) to bring together insights from a number of different positions in linguistics and language education and bring them to bear on the curricular conundrum of what constitutes knowledge about language and how this knowledge may contribute to children's language development, not least in learning how to read.

It may be useful, however, before looking at what the LINC pack has to say about reading, to set the context. The LINC (Language in the National Curriculum) programme was a government-funded training programme intended to disseminate the model of language described in the Kingman Report and to support the introduction of the National Curriculum in English. The programme ran from 1989 to 1992 and, unusually for such grant-aided programmes, covered every local authority in England and Wales.

The brief given to the programme's academic director, Professor Ronald Carter of Nottingham University, was to prepare a pack of in-service materials and to train approximately twenty six regional co-ordinators who then undertook the dissemination of the programme to secondary English teachers and primary language co-ordinators throughout their areas. Higher Education institutions were not included in the programme's targets, although the need to involve them in the dissemination of the Kingman model of language was specially recommended in that report.

It should be stressed that the programme did not include any research element, nor was any time allotted for Professor Carter to investigate what was virtually a new curriculum area, that of knowledge about language over and above the traditional conception of this as grammar, spelling and punctuation. It was expected that this would all be achieved within the three month period allowed for the training of co-ordinators.

In the event the materials - a printed pack of in-service activities and some audio-visual materials - were devised by the director and co-ordinators working together with contributions from the many advisory and classroom teachers who quickly became involved in the extensive in-service programme which absorbed most of the programme's funding. There was much debate among everyone involved about what knowledge should be developed and/or taught. Providing a pedagogical framework for Kingman's essentially descriptive account of language turned out to be far from easy and, as always, the close connection between language and thought made it difficult to determine where the role of language in education ceased.

Nevertheless, the materials were completed roughly two years after the beginning of the programme in the expectation that they would be issued by the then Department of Education to all schools so that published, rather than draft, materials could be used in the final phase of training.

The rest, as they say, is history. This is not the place to describe in detail the complex political debate which quickly surrounded LINC's attempts to persuade the Department that the materials were both necessary and suitable to their purpose and that the programme's success had been jeopardised by their non-publication. What is of interest in the context of current debates about reading and moves to alter National Curriculum requirements in English, is that the disagreements centred on the same issues that apparently now threaten the "Cox" curriculum: to what extent should language teaching methods be based in children's own language use and how far should a single variety of language dominate school-based learning?

While the LINC materials are very far from suggesting an "anything goes" approach to language teaching, they clearly threaten authoritarian notions of teaching and the imposition of "correct" models of language. They assume, for example, that children must from the beginning have access to the range of literacy skills which empower sophisticated readers and writers, that the provenance of reading material should extend far beyond that of a traditional canon of literature, and that children's language development in school should support the experimental nature of natural language acquisition.

None of these ideas is, of course, particularly novel or outrageous and it is interesting to note the incredulity voiced by foreign observers of the LINC debate when they first see these supposedly controversial materials. Viewed from outside the current political context they seem quite unthreatening. The major criticism of LINC might rather be that its challenging of so-called traditional views of language education is somewhat diffuse and inconclusive; what might once have been thought of as typically British compromise.

Yet within their own context, the LINC materials do constitute the same kind of threat to authoritarian notions of control that the current National Curriculum English Orders present. This is immediately apparent in the units relating to reading. Essential to the thinking here is that, as with all language use, neither the act of reading nor the text with which the reader engages is either neutral or immutable. Language is seen as essentially meaningful and dynamic, with readers bringing to texts their own understandings including their knowledge of other texts and of the cultures which produced them. Yet the systematic nature of language is not ignored. The existence of a common code for the written word provides the groundwork for the negotiation which must occur when reader and text meet: both author and reader have much to play with but each has also to respect the constraints which the language code imposes including the values, expectations and cultural histories loaded onto it by successive readers.

The very fabric of the written grammar is itself reflective of social and cultural roles, often indicating assumed or covert power relationships. For example, the use of the passive, the present tense and the universal singular in information texts all reflect an expectation that the text will not be called in question, that what is said is true and unchanging, that there is no single person with her own perspective and prejudices who is responsible for this text. The LINC view is that texts can never be neutral and that the positions of readers and authors must be explored before texts yield up their meanings. In declaring that language can manipulate and deceive as well as inform and liberate, LINC envisages readers who may lose a certain innocence in acquiring literacy skills but who are, as a result, truly enfranchised.

While this may be heady stuff to some, it is hardly new. What the writers of the LINC units on reading have done is to support the National Curriculum in English in expanding the reading curriculum and making it text and meaning centred. In doing so, they have drawn on the insights of ethnography and stylistics as well as on Halliday's discourse driven model of language. A pedagogy of reading is suggested here in which - admittedly incompletely - both the idea of the active reader and the importance of textual features to successful reading are recognised. Essential to these understandings is that features of code and text are not barriers to be overcome but sources of evidence for the construction of meaning.

The recognition that an understanding of the structure of texts is necessary to successful language use lies behind the two-fold division of the three LINC 'modal' units (those on Talk, Reading and Writing) into those aspects of the mode which concern the user's engagement (PROCESS) and those which relate to the characteristics of a range of texts (REPERTOIRE). Thus the unit on the reading process includes activities and commentaries relating to the purposes of reading, cultural perceptions of literacy and readers' and writers' prior knowledge and assumptions, as well as considering aspects of decoding.

Interestingly, it is here that DARTs-type activities are included, rather than in the Repertoire unit. What the LINC authors seem to be saying here is that making sense of a text involves seeing how it coheres internally, as well as externally in relation to its context of production. Again, the knowledge of language brought into play is not new but the juxtapositioning of activities relating to decoding and to the uncovering of textual organisation suggests an interesting and productive approach to dealing with progression in reading.

The Repertoire unit is thus freed to consider specific features of a range of texts to which a generalised reading process rooted in knowledge about language can be applied. This is to depart from an approach to reading which suggests that particular texts require discrete reading skills while still recognising that different texts presume different kinds of language understanding in their readers. Implicit here is an understanding that neither the reading process nor texts themselves can be thought of as hierarchically ordered: children reading a picture book with an adult are expected to bring to bear their knowledge of other texts and their own experience of life as well as their knowledge of how a story is structured.

Inevitably, there are criticisms which can be levelled at the LINC reading units, not least that, as in much of the rest of the materials, the lack of an explanatory overview of the kind briefly attempted here makes some omissions hard to understand. For example, knowing that the material is constituted not as a reading course but as support for the construction of one, suggests why the teaching of phonics has such a low profile since this is an area commonly covered in reading scheme manuals. Nevertheless, young children's knowledge about language includes an understanding of letters and sounds, and word recognition, and approaches to the teaching of these might usefully have been included, perhaps drawing on the work of Holdaway. Again, in looking at how readers and texts interact, there is little opportunity to consider the position of writers, including children's own experience of authorship. The LINC approach is, rightly, a text-centred one but in considering how readers meet texts, it is surely important that the engagement of authors should also be considered.

It was suggested at the beginning of this article that it is the thinking behind the LINC materials, rather than their use, which will in the end make a significant contribution to language education. LINC's major influence in the last three years has in any case been channelled through the in-service programmes which had to run for most of that time either independently or with piece-meal materials culled from draft documents. This informal and diffuse influence appears to be continuing in some places, with in-service and initial reading courses currently being constructed to include LINC insights as well as using some of the activities from the materials. There must now be many teachers and children who started deconstructing texts, from crisp packets to history text books, after someone came back from a LINC course. There are others who have welcomed the opportunity to develop in children a vastly increased range of reading skills using a wide variety of "ordinary' books and texts. If these practices are threatening to standards of reading, and to language development in general, it will be interesting to see what effective substitutes are in store for us.

Both writers were employed as part of the LINC training programme in the period 1989-1992. Neither contributed to the writing of the LINC reading units. The views expressed here are entirely their own.

Being a Whole Language Teacher in the United States

Katherine Davies Samway
Lucinda Pease-Alvarez

In the United States, reading instruction frequently relies heavily on textbooks and teacher-led lessons that introduce children to small parts of language (e.g. short vowels, beginning consonants). Children are then required to practice these subskills on worksheets. In this type of skills-based program, reading is not viewed as an interaction between the reader and the text, or as an opportunity to read for enjoyment and/or gain knowledge about interesting topics.

In the past ten years, many teachers in the United States have moved away from this type of skills-based, teacher and textbook-directed curriculum to more student-centred and meaning-oriented approaches to learning and teaching. These educators often refer to themselves as whole language teachers (e.g. Goodman, Goodman & Bird, 1990; Samway & Alvarez 1987). Although the move towards whole language teaching in the United States is frequently viewed as a grass roots movement since it is often teachers who are enthusiastic advocates for programmatic and pedagogical changes, these teachers have been influenced, either directly or indirectly, by the work of researcher/teacher educators (e.g. Goodman, Smith, Meredith & Goodman, 1987; Harste, Woodward & Burke, 1984).

Investigating Variations in the Pedagogical Perspectives of Whole Language Teachers

As professors in teacher education programs, we work closely with self-described whole language teachers, and we have noticed that the term, whole language, means quite different things according to the person with whom we are talking. For example, in some cases the term refers to a particular learning activity (e.g., using 'big books', oversized books with predictable elements). In other cases, it refers to a teacher's philosophy of teaching. We have also noticed that these same teachers are often attacked by their colleagues for their non-traditional teaching practices. In order to more fully understand what it means to be a whole language teacher in the United States in the early 1990s, we embarked on a research project designed to: (a) assess trends in how whole language is understood and implemented by those who identify themselves as whole language teachers, and (b) identify ways in which teachers may be supported as they move towards meaning-based, whole language approaches to learning and teaching.

We interviewed 47 elementary teachers in Northern California. The teachers came from 20 schools (urban, suburban, and rural) in seven school districts. Although we

181

asked a standard set of questions (e.g. What influenced you to become a whole language teacher? For you, what does the term 'whole language' mean?), the interviews were open-ended and we followed up with probing questions. In the following pages we will discuss some of our preliminary findings.

The Teachers and Their Teaching Contexts

Most of the teachers have been teaching for at least five years. Three of the twenty schools in which they work have designated themselves as whole language schools. Unlike non-whole language schools, the majority of the teachers and administrators at these schools advocate a whole language approach to instruction, and implement instructional practices that they believe are consistent with this approach.

The professional contexts in which the teachers work vary a great deal. At some schools relationships among the staff are cordial and friendly. Many teachers, however, complained of having to work in a setting fraught with conflict and divisiveness. For example, one teacher talked openly about how whole language had been an issue that divided the staff at her school:

Our staff, unfortunately, is a very divided one. We have a lot of older teachers that are very much into decoding skills and traditional strategies. And we have about more than half of our staff that has been new in the past five years, so you have a lot of new (name of local university) students that are trying to incorporate whole language activities ... So there's unfortunately two different groups at our school: one that would like to keep it more traditional and one that would like to engage in more hands-on activities.

Becoming a Whole Language Teacher

In the United States, the preparation for becoming a teacher usually begins after completing a four-year undergraduate degree program. Teacher education programs do not usually last for more than one year (two full semesters and a summer), and tend to consist of general background courses (e.g. social and psychological foundations of education), teaching methods courses (language arts, science, mathematics, social studies), and a teaching practice. Upon successful completion of this program, students receive a teaching credential.

What was very striking when we looked at the data was the fact that very few of the teachers had been introduced to whole language through a pre-service programme. Some teachers even commented that they had to unlearn what they had been taught in their pre-service programmes. This suggests that their teacher education programmes are not up-to-date in terms of current theory and practice. The majority of teachers learned about whole language as practising teachers. Some teachers talked of their own boredom with and disinterest in teaching, and their search for a teaching approach that would cause children to become more engaged learners and result in them becoming more enthusiastic teachers. Some teachers were introduced to whole language through knowledgeable colleagues, conference presentations, consultants, nationally known experts, and reading.

All of the teachers commented on how being a whole language teacher is an on-going process, and they are anxious to increase their knowledge base. In many cases, the teachers have initiated their own continuing professional development. They commented on how little support they receive from their districts, even though they find that it requires more time and energy to be a whole language teacher. The teachers often experience tremendous professional isolation and do not believe that enough training has been and is being provided for them. When we asked them about the kind of professional development opportunities they felt would be most useful, the teachers had concrete suggestions:

(a) time to read, think, observe, and talk with other teachers,
(b) professional books and journals in their schools,
(c) long-term staff development opportunities, and
(d) peer coaching for teachers who are new to whole language.

Definitions of Whole Language

The teachers' definitions of whole language fall into three general categories: (a) one that emphasizes instructional activities and events, (b) one that emphasizes how children learn, and (c) one that emphasizes a socio-political view of teaching.

An instructional view of whole language

Preliminary analysis suggests that most of the teachers view whole language as an instructional program, a cluster of teaching methods, or a curricular innovation. Their definitions emphasize what goes on in the classroom. The following excerpt is an example of this view:

To me it's a language arts program, it's not a reading program, and it's using all the aspects of listening and writing and reading. It's not a programme that's phonics-based in which everybody starts, and this is 'A' week and we all study 'A' - do dittos on 'A'. That's what it's not. It's a program where the children have a chance to use language in singing, interacting, and they immediately feel successful as readers because they have books that they've memorized that are simple books with a repetitive patterning. It's just a program that children can feel successful (with) from the very beginning. And no matter what their ability.

The teachers frequently referred to instructional practices such as writers' workshop, shared reading/big book/frame writing, thematic instruction, and reading trade books.

Whole language as a theory of learning

Definitions that fall in this category frequently refer to the need to ground practices in the needs of children (i.e. student-centred teaching). In the excerpt below, the teacher emphasizes the role of oral language development and argues that learning language and literacy is a natural process that parallels the way children learn to speak:

It's based, I think, a lot on the model of the way that we acquire oral language, which is not by teaching a child to speak in a certain way. It's like if a child says, 'Mi, mi?' you say, 'Oh you want milk? Okay here's some milk,' You pour 'em some milk. You don't say, 'Oh, no. You have to say, 'Please pass the milk." Traditionally, we have thought that language has to be taught that way because they have to know it all before they can use it correctly, you know. And whole language is kind of like - you use it, you play with it, you have fun with it. You make mistakes. You make a lot of mistakes, but it's like developmental. The language process is developmental, and by teaching skills in abstract little units you hinder the learning process because here the kids are trying to use this language system to explain, you know, as a tool, and if you break it down it's like it doesn't make sense to 'em.

Sometimes, the interviews revealed a rather dogmatic stance toward theory. For example, one teacher evaluated instructional approaches by determining whether or not they are compatible with her theoretical orientation about whole language, rather than whether they met the needs of her students.

Socio-political view of teaching

Only two teachers defined whole language in relation to the socio-political context in which they live and work. Linda, who has a 12-year history as a whole language teacher, provides a definition that challenges traditional views about the role of students and teachers in schools.

It's very freeing in some ways. It's not that you don't ever tend to things anymore, it's just that you tend to them while people are getting their feet on the ground, while people are getting the information that they need, and then you pull away and you let people do what it is they're going to do. It's not that you're giving them power, because everybody has that. It's just that you're acknowledging what they already have. I think in terms of the whole, you know, the political world, that it makes me take another look at what's going on around me in the world and recognizing ways that those kinds of things can be brought into the classroom ... It's kind of your philosophy of life after a whole. It is very political ... it's the political kind of thing that makes you say, 'I wonder why we need a principal. Aren't there things that we can do for ourselves?' I hate the word empowering, but I think what happens to teachers is that they do become more aware of the fact that they do have a lot of power, you know, in a good kind of way, not in a negative way. But they do know. I think a lot of teachers don't really know how much they know.

Problems Teachers have with Whole Language

In our interviews, we asked teachers to discuss the difficulties they have with whole language. Most teachers commented that they did not have a problem with whole language per se, but they mentioned problems they have with the way that whole language is interpreted by others. Several teachers commented that a lot of myths circulate about whole language, making it difficult to work in an environment that can often become hostile. One teacher wondered if the term had outlived its usefulness, possibly leading to complacency on the part of some self-described whole language teachers, and undermining other teachers who find it hard to live up to the ideals. Some teachers remarked on the added burden of teaching children who are not familiar with 'whole language materials and activities' and sometimes resist taking responsibility for their learning.

Some of our respondents were critical of whole language peers who they believe take a laissez-faire approach to instruction that does not meet the academic needs of their students. For example, a veteran teacher, Gina, who works in a predominantly Mexican-American suburban neighbourhood, criticized her colleagues 'free-form' approach to teaching. She worries that some of her colleagues are relinquishing their responsibility as teachers:

Just chaos isn't whole language. Non-structure isn't whole language. Lack of teaching and intervening and being involved with kids is not whole language. Sitting back and letting it happen isn't whole language. Saying spelling isn't important isn't whole language. Saying , 'Well it's developmental; maybe they'll get it next year,' isn't whole language. That's just an irresponsible teacher.

Implications for Teacher Education

It was not easy for most of the teachers to articulate their thinking, and several commented that this was the first time that they had ever been asked to talk about these issues, or about their teaching stances and practices in general. Many teachers commented that they were figuring out what they believed as they talked with us. We believe that teachers (and prospective teachers) should be given many opportunities to explore and develop their philosophical stances and pedagogies in order to be as successful as possible when working with children. With greater thoughtfulness, it is more likely that teachers will generate and integrate theory and practice.

It is clear that these self-described whole language teachers do not share a single definition of whole language. However, very few teachers referred to how children learn when articulating their view of whole language; those that did had generally worked closely with whole language theorists who have done extensive research on how children learn language and literacy (e.g. Carole Edelsky, Ken Goodman, Yetta Goodman and Jerome Harste). Because effective teaching requires one to carefully balance student needs and learning processes with instructional practices, we are concerned that so many teachers articulated a definition of whole language that focused on instructional practices only. Based on our extensive experience in teacher education, we would like to offer some explanations for this phenomenon.

Poorly designed classes in teacher education programmes

In many teacher education programmes theory and practice classes are taught separately, thereby undermining the notion that practice and theory inform each other. There is considerable pressure on teachers of methods courses to give prospective teachers the 'tricks of the trade' and gloss over related theoretical issues. In addition, because of the few months devoted to preparing to be a teacher, teacher educators in the United States have a very limited amount of time in which to explore reading instruction with student teachers (often meeting for only three to six hours a week for one semester). In many instances the methods classes are not connected with a school experience period so that the learning is removed from actual classrooms and students.

'Shot-in-the-dark' format of many in-service programmes

When teachers encounter whole language in their staff development programmes, it is likely that their introduction will be oriented more to classroom practices than the whys of classroom practices. In the United Stages, staff development for teachers often consists of short sessions held after school. Only rarely are these sessions part of a series that explores a single issue. Because of the limited time devoted to staff development and the fragmented nature of topics under discussion, it is inevitable that knowledge about children's learning processes (the theory) is passed over in favour of teaching activities. Our own experiences as teacher educators in these kinds of situations remind us of how difficult it is to delve into the whys of what we do as teachers when teachers are tired by the end of the day and are anxious for teaching activities that they can implement the next day. This reality is supported, in large measure, by school systems that do not implement in-service programmes that encourage teachers to think critically about their pedagogy.

Teacher education programmes in the United States, at either the higher education or local district level, do not tend to emphasize explorations into why we do what we do as teachers. Programmes are often atheoretical and teachers are not viewed as potential or actual generators of theory. Instead, teachers are frequently regarded as the implementors of instructional programmes (many of which are packaged and unrelated to student needs). In the interviews, teacher after teacher argued for more thoughtful teacher preparation and in-service programmes, with opportunities to reflect upon their practice and the learning of their students.

References

GOODMAN, K.S., GOODMAN, Y., & BIRD L.B. (Eds) (1990). *The Whole Language Catalog*. New York: Random House

GOODMAN, K.S., SMITH, E.B., MEREDITH, R. & GOODMAN, Y.M. (1987). *Language and Thinking in School: A Whole-Language Curriculum*. 3rd edition. New York: Richard C. Owen Publishers

HARSTE, J.C., WOODWARD, V.A., & BURKE, C.L. (1984). *Language Stories and Literacy Lessons*. Portsmouth, NH: Heinemann Educational Books

SAMWAY, K.D., & ALVAREZ, L.P. (1987) 'Integrating Language Arts Instruction for Language Minority Students.' *educational Horizons*. 66(1), 20-24

Balancing Perspectives in the Teaching of Literacy: Professional Texts in a Critical Context

Roger Beard

Recent years have seen debates about the teaching of literacy become unduly polarised and sometimes over reliant on slogans and 'sound bites'. Opposing views have often been caricatured and a number of influential publications seem to have omitted altogether references to evidence (or sometimes the lack of it) which are not compatible with their theoretical position. There has been a surprising lack of debate in professional publications to bring issues and evidence together in a more balanced way.

This paper will concentrate on debates about early reading development, although there will be a brief mention of writing. The paper has been structured to link with the seminal work of Marilyn Jager Adams (1990) to highlight the main practical implications which stem from her remarkably assiduous review of research in *Beginning to Read*. Marilyn Adams' simple model of the reading process indicates the integral relationships between meaning, letters and sounds within a specific context.

Figure 1: Modelling the reading system: Four processors

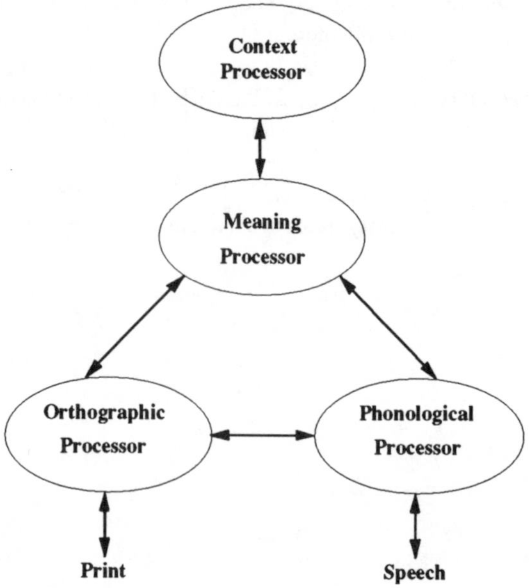

188

What follows in this paper is intended to balance some of the excessive assertions of the recent past and to contribute to the reappraisal of the literacy teaching in primary education called for in the discussion paper *Curriculum Organisation and Classroom Practice in Primary Schools* (DES, 1992), so that we may be duly watchful for 'highly questionable dogmas' and 'excessively complex classroom practices' and ensure that literacy is 'taught effectively' (DES, 1992 p.1).

Whole Language and Literacy Learning

In beginning with the central focus on meaning, we need to ask fundamental questions about our mechanisms for making meaning by the use of literacy. Children need to learn about relationships between spoken and written language in a number of ways. The linguistic relationships are indicated in the models of language in, for instance, the Kingman Report (DES, 1988) and David Crystal's work (Crystal, 1987). However, it may be misleading to assume that the learning of literacy involves similar psychological processes to those involved in learning spoken language, as has been suggested in the so-called 'whole language' perspective. In fact, the phrase 'whole language' is itself problematic. A recent chapter by Marilyn Adams (1991) reports a survey of 64 articles in which the phrase was used. Of the two-thirds which offered definitions, there were marked differences: 'whole language' was variously defined as an approach, a philosophy, an orientation, a theory, a perspective and an attitude of mind. No 'focal attributes' were cited by two-thirds of the definitions. In the United Kingdom the phrase seems to be used to refer to teaching approaches which exploit the reciprocal relationships between the four language modes. But this is very different from assuming that the psychological processes of literacy learning are closely similar to those of learning the mother tongue, an assumption shared by several influential sources including Kenneth Goodman (1986), Liz Waterland (1988, pp 12-14) and the former Inner London Education Authority's *Primary Language Record* (ILEA, 1988, p.23). Margaret Donaldson (1989) has been particularly concerned to argue that literacy learning is a profoundly different enterprise from the learning of our mother tongue. Reading and writing involve the use of an arbitrary, symbolic system. We are not biologically equipped to communicate with these symbols in the way in which we are equipped to speak and listen.

Jessie Reid (1993) also points out the limitations of the related suggestion (by Kenneth Goodman and others) that fluent reading involves predicting sequences and checking them 'against the most productive cues'. She refers to studies which suggest that written language is not as predictable as Goodman seems to assume, even though we may feel it is when taking part in cloze procedure in which individual words are deleted but where the surrounding text is visible. However when all the following text is deleted (so-called 'blind cloze') the success rate in cloze procedure falls drastically. The use of context cues is obviously helpful to beginning readers but, for fluent readers, optimally efficient reading seems more to depend on fast, almost unconscious word recognition, in which 'expectancy', rather than 'prediction' plays a supportive role. She argues that the very novelty and constant creativity of written language make it largely *un*predictable. In the recurrent top down - bottom up controversy about how we read, Jessie Reid makes a strong case for reading being 'interactive, with bottom-up priority'.

Emergent Literacy and 'Submergent' Literacy

As I indicated in my earlier book (Beard, 1990) there are a number of perspectives on early literacy, concerned with measurable skills ('reading readiness'), awareness ('cognitive clarity') and text-based behaviours ('emergent reading'). In recent years, there have been arguments that the latter is the most appropriate notion for the phase of development before fluent reading is established. This is an appealing perspective, as it indicates that learning about literacy does not begin at the age of 5 or at nine in the morning, but gradually, in a variety of contexts, in which the purpose and uses of literacy become appreciated. But there are questionable assumptions in some of the work in this field.

Two major contributors on this topic, William Teale and Elizabth Sulzby (1986, pp vii-xxv) assume that language learning and literacy learning are psychologically similar but, as was shown above, this is a highly contentious view. In fact, there are several other uncertainties and questions about the emerging literacy perspective, including the adequacy of the notion itself, its manifestations in how children's skills develop over time and in the ethnographic research approaches which are often used to investigate it.

One important uncertainty is the lack of an underlying framework to explain why, in some instances, literacy development remains 'submerged'. Barbara Tizard's (1988) research into 33 inner city schools, for example, found that, of the 93 children whose reading at the end of infant school was very poor, only seven had made any spurt in progress a year later. Indeed, children who made little progress during one year in the infant school usually made little progress in the next.

There are also questions about how the emergence of literacy is manifested in children's writing. The most eminent British researcher into spelling, Margaret Peters (1985), has expressed concern that the 'nebulous' concept of 'inventive spelling' may become associated with an assumption that children will 'catch' spelling incidentally, whereas her own research suggests that children's success in spelling in the primary years has generally more to do with the influence of what teachers do than any other factor, especially in helping children to attend to patterns in spelling, to develop a visual memory and a swift and well-formed style of handwriting.

Similarly, a leading British specialist in the study of children's handwriting has warned that 'Reception teachers must not be encouraged to ignore movement errors that soon become automatic, leading to serious problems. This vital early teaching should start as soon as children try to write' (Sassoon, 1989, p. B3).

Such cautions can be linked to the perennial problem in ethnographic research regarding the 'reality' it seeks to convey (Hammersley 1992), for the very process by which observers interpret and define children's early 'literacy acts' demands interpretation and explanation in itself. The significance of scribbles, invented spellings and guesses at the meaning of print is not necessarily self-evident and attempts to explain it can conceivably refer to behaviour and comprehension which may eventually prove to be inefficient and misleading, even as approximations, and which the children may themselves in time disown.

Teachers may therefore need to balance a sensitivity to how literacy emerges with a commitment actively to ensure that long-term learning difficulties are prevented, as the originator of the notion of 'emergent literacy', Marie Clay (1982) herself, has argued.

Perhaps the most serious omission in many publications on the emergent literacy is specific mention of auditory factors in early literacy development and yet weaknesses in this area have often been found to be evident in delayed reading development (see for instance Bryant and Bradley, 1985, and their use of reading age-match designs to allow for differences in literacy experience). This takes us to the need to balance shared reading and attention to the code itself.

Shared Reading and Attention to the Code itself

Recent years have seen a great increase in interest in various approaches to shared reading, of which the best known is the 'apprenticeship approach' (Waterland, 1988). This recognises the importance of reading to and with children from an early age, agreed as the single most important thing we can do to promote children's reading by major government-funded reports on both sides of the Atlantic (DES, 1975, p.97; Adams, 1990, p.86). There are, however, serious flaws in some of Liz Waterland's arguments, of which the most important is the lack of attention to the nature of the code itself. There are also uncertainties over several of her other arguments, one of which was referred to above, in relation to the parallels between language and literacy development. She also draws heavily on the work of Frank

Smith and Kenneth Goodman and thus is open to similar criticisms in relation to their view of fluent reading as a process of checking predictions or guesses, a view which has now been discredited (Adams, 1991). She also seems unnecessarily to wed her teaching approach exclusively to 'real books' (or 'organic' or 'free range' books). Moreover, her list of children's reading behaviours, from successive sharing of an attractive and rewarding book, seems to be 'locked in' to that one book.

Publications on shared reading are generally weaker on how children's learning experiences from one book are consolidated for use in another. Beyond the 'directional' learning (Clay, 1972) of how books work, the vocabulary, syntax, structure and register of books are largely unpredictable, with their meaning often depending disproportionately on unfamiliar words, especially in non-narrative books, as Marilyn Adams (1991) points out (see also Littlefair, 1991). This would seem to be a good reason, in principle, for the use of some form of reading scheme or series of books, but I will come to this issue later.

Waterland seems to overlook the fact that what is predictable from one book to another in written English is the use of the alphabetic system. This was specifically developed to represent the phonemes of spoken language and therefore to make it economical and productive compared with logographic and other writing systems in which thousands of different characters have to be learned separately. The apprenticeship approach as set out by Waterland (1988, pp.34-5) is surely seriously misleading in her suggestion that children need to use strategies based primarily on two questions: one (overtly first, unconsciously later) 'What is this word likely to be?' and two 'Does the word begin with the letter or couple of letters that it should if I am right?' ... 'More than this is largely unnecessary for reading'.

Waterland suggests that these two questions are all that are needed to read 'new words'. But this raises the question as to how children learn some words in the first place which, of course, provide the cues for reading other words. She suggests (p.35) that 'phonic understanding ... is only one very small part of reading'. Is she therefore suggesting that children learn to read entirely logographically? Various psychological 'stage models suggest that many children may begin to read this way (Oakhill, 1993), but that their progress towards independent reading can be greatly speeded by being helped to attend to the alphabetic structure of English (see Adams, 1990).

The need to address both the sharing of reading and the structure of written language is reflected in Vygotsky's contribution to the field. His suggestions on collaborative learning and the importance of the 'zone of proximal development' are now regularly brought in to various theories on literacy learning. These suggestions from *Mind in Society* (1978) may be easier to apply to the learning of practical tasks (as with those studied by Edwards and Mercer, 1987). Vygotsky's suggestions on literacy learning are set out in greater detail in *Thought and Language* (1962). Here he stressed the abstract, symbolic nature of writing and the necessity for learners to develop a kind of 'linguistic awareness' of its structure in relation to speech, because 'written speech' is a separate linguistic function, differing from oral speech in both structure and mode of functioning.

As I said earlier, in English, this structure is based on its phonemic system; we change meanings by changing how a phoneme is represented (bit-bat; must-mist). According to David Crystal (1990), the great majority of English words are patterned in this way. The genuinely irregular words tend to be very common, Anglo-Saxon words ('are', 'once', 'was'). Venezky's scholarly analysis of English orthography led him to conclude that his 'classification scheme for spelling to sound patterns ... could be used as a basis for the selection of words in the teaching of reading' (Venezky, 1970,p.128).

But this does not necessarily imply an endorsement of 'phonics first and fast' in the teaching of early reading. As well as the historical irregularities mentioned above, it is not as easy to detect the phonemic structure of a word as some might argue. How many phonemes are represented in *string*? If we find it difficult to separate the phonemes from the 'acoustic stream' of speech, then young children obviously will.

Important work on children's phonological development has been done for some years by Peter Bryant and his colleagues at Oxford (e.g. Goswami and Bryant, 1990). Although he has not subscribed to a 'stage theory' of reading development, he does offer important insights into how children's awareness of the sounds of language may develop:
- awareness of syllables: string
- awareness of intra-syllabic units (onset and rime): str ing c.f. s ing or br ing
- awareness of phonemes : /s/t/r/i/ng.

Bryant, like Adams, stresses how this learning can be promoted particularly effectively by the use of entertaining and informative books, especially those which reflect our heritage of rhymes, alliteration, I-spy and word play.

This brings us to the reading schemes - real books debate and the contexts which they provide for literacy learning.

Real books and reading scheme books

The debates about the greater use of picture books in the teaching of reading have highlighted the importance of the quality of texts used in the teaching of reading. The Cox Report summarised this increased awareness by stressing that the criteria for selecting books should include considerations of print, illustrations, paper and binding, language, plot and child appeal (DES, 1989, p.28).

These words build upon the more searching literary and psychological studies of what makes a 'good book' for children, from writers such as Nicholas Tucker (1981, 1993).

This exhortation can inspire teachers to make the most of the 'golden age' of children's picture books, using them to enrich a school's book provision, according them similar status to scheme books by the purchase of multiple copies, using their polysemic qualities across the curriculum and not overlooking their potential for showing children how the code 'works', in ways suggested above.

The mistake is to combine these practices with a caricatured rejection of reading schemes. For scheme books increasingly embody the features outlined by Cox and they have the curiously overlooked strength of consolidating links between books for young learners. (In fact there is a similarity here between the ways spoken language and reading can be supported - by a shared, continuing context and consciously limited vocabulary! See Perera, 1993).

Ironically, there is almost tacit support for these conclusions in the work of Margaret Meek and her colleagues (1983) despite their avowed eschewal of the use of scheme books. Rather surprisingly, Meek admits to basing her ambitious theories about 'how texts teach what readers learn' on treating anecdotes as evidence (Meek, 1988, p.8). Even more surprisingly, she refers the dubious reader of her work, who may find her arguments too 'impressionistic', to an earlier book (Meek et al, 1983) in which she says 'We gave them real books and showed them how texts teach' (Meek, 1988, p.40). But when we turn to the earlier book, we read that the inexperienced adolescents did not learn to read, apparently because the teacher researchers had come to them 'too late' (Meek et al, 1983, p.223). Yet if we turn to p.164, we find a transcript from the reflections of one of the teachers in the project coming desperately close to admitting that the learners may have benefited from the support of some kind of reading scheme, a possibility which Margaret Meek and her colleagues seemed, nevertheless, to avoid on principle:

'S: I find exactly this the problem right at the hub of it, moving from the known to the unknown and the independence of being able to pick up a book and just reading it without knowing about it ... all the time you come back and say, how can I ease that transition ... how can you, instead of suddenly whipping away a whole chunk of support from underneath, "now we're going to try something new", how do you *gradually take it away brick by brick. I've said this before and never completely resolved it.'* (from Meek et al 1983, p.164).

Balancing Perspectives in the Teaching of Literacy

This last quotation highlights how the perennial debates about the teaching and learning of literacy can at times be over-polarised, how references to research and publications can be insufficiently eclectic and how, in these pressured times, the heart may sometimes overrule the head.

Marilyn Adams's model reminds us that reading involves making meaning by linking our perceptions of letters and sounds in a specific context. A different sense of context is important when we look at professional texts in the field, which can be in danger of reflecting a certain ideology rather than providing the kind of broad and balanced synthesis which befits professionalism and may optimally benefit children learning to read.

Panaceas for universal literacy, even in advanced industrialised societies, do not seem imminent. Until they are, it behoves us to be cautious, critical and reflective, seeking evidence above the slogans and the sound bites.

I am grateful to Peter Daw of Suffolk LEA for the reminder of how Tennyson's words can inform the context of continuing debates: 'There lives more faith in honest doubt, believe me, than in half the creeds'.

References

ADAMS, M.J. (1990) *Beginning to Read: Thinking and Learning about Print.* Cambridge, Mass.: MIT Press

ADAMS, M.J. (1991) 'Why not phonics and whole langage?' in Ellis, W. (Ed) *All Language and the Creation and Literacy.* Baltimore, M.D.: The Orton Dyslexia Society

BEARD, R. (1990) *Developing Reading 3-13* (Second Edition). Sevenoaks: Hodder and Stoughton

BEARD, R. (Ed) (1993) *Teaching Literacy: Balancing Perspectives.* London: Hodder and Stoughton

BRYANT, P.E. AND BRADLEY, L. (1985) *Children's Reading Problems.* Oxford: Basil Blackwell

CLAY, M.M. (1972) *Reading: The Patterning of Complex Behaviour.* London: Heinemann Educational Books

CLAY, M.M. (1982) *Observing Young Readers.* Exeter, N. H.: Heinemann

CRYSTAL, D. (1987) *Child Language, Learning and Linguistics* (Second Edition). London: Edward Arnold

CRYSTAL, D. (1990) *The English Language.* Harmondsworth: Penguin Books

DES (1975) *A Language for Life* (The Bullock Report). London: HMSO

DES (1988) *Report of the Committee of Enquiry into the Teachng of English Language* (The Kingman Report). London: HMSO

DES (1989) *English for ages 5-16: National Curriculum Proposals of the Secretary of State for Education and Science and the Secretary of State for Wales* (The Cox Report). London: HMSO

DES (1992) *Curriculum Organistion and Classroom Practice in Primary Schools: A Discussion Paper by Robin Alexander, Jim Rose, and Chris Woodhead.* London: DES Information Branch

DONALDSON, M., (1989) *Sense and Sensibility: Some thoughts on the teaching of literacy* (Occasional Paper No 3). Reading: Reading and Language Information Centre, University of Reading (reprinted in Beard, (1993) *op cit*)

EDWARDS, D. AND MERCER, N. (1987) *Common Knowledge.* London: Methuen.

GOODMAN, K. (1986) *What's Whole in Whole Language?* Ontario: Scholastic Publications

GOSWAMI, U. AND BRYANT, P.E. (1990) *Phonological Skills and Learning to Read.* Hove: Lawrence Erlbaum Associates

HAMMERSLEY, M. (1992) *What's Wrong with Ethnography?* London: Routledge

INNER LONDON EDUCATION AUTHORITY (1988) *The Primary Language Record.* London: Centre for Language in Primary Education

LITTLEFAIR, A. (1991) *Reading All Types of Writing.* Buckingham: Open University Press.

MEEK, M. et al (1983) *Achieving Literacy.* London: Routledge and Kegan Paul

MEEK, M. (1988) *How Texts Teach What Readers Learn.* Stroud: Thimble Press

OAKHILL, J.V. (1993) 'Developing Skilled Reading' in Beard (1993) *op cit*

PERERA, K. (1993) 'The Good Book: Linguistic Aspects' in Beard (1993) *op cit*

PETERS, M.L. (1985) *Spelling Caught or Taught? A New Look.* London: Routledge and Kegan Paul

REID, J.F. (1993) 'Reading and Spoken Language: The Nature of the Links' in Beard (1993) *op cit*

SASSOON, R. (1989) 'You've got to Hand it to Them', *TES* 17th February

TEALE, W. AND SULZBY, E. (Eds) (1986) *Emergent Literacy: Writing and Reading.* Norwood, N.J.: Ablex Publ.Co.

TIZARD, B. et al (1988) *Young Children at School in the Inner City.* London: Lawrence Erlbaum Associates

TUCKER, N. (1981) *The Child and the Book.* Cambridge University Press

TUCKER, N. (1993) 'The Good Book: Literary and Developmental Aspects' in Beard (1993) *op cit*

VENEZKY, R.L. (1970) *The Structure of English Orthography.* The Hague: Mouton

VYGOTSKY, L.S. (1962) *Thought and Language.* Cambridge, Mass.: MIT Press

VYGOTSKY, L.S. (1978) *Mind in Society.* (Trans. Cole, M. et al) Cambridge, Mass: Harvard University Press

WATERLAND, L. (1988) *Read With Me: An Apprenticeship Approach to Reading* (Second Edition). Stroud: Thimble Press

List of contributors

John Aldridge is a Past President of The Newspaper Society.

Roger Beard is Lecturer in Education at the University of Leeds.

Sara Brody is the Director of the Educational Disabilities and Reading Graduate Program at Rivier College, New Hampshire.

Margaret Cook is General Adviser (Early Years) for Sefton M.B.C.

Katharine Davies Samway works in the School of Education, San Jose State University, California

Ros Fisher is a lecturer at the University of Plymouth in Exmouth.

Rebecca Huss works at the University of Houston Clear Lake in Houston, Texas.

Jeff Hynds is an educational consultant and in-service course leader in Biggin Hill, Kent.

Sylvia Karavis is a language advisory teacher in Oxfordshire.

Bob Leather works at the Lake District campus of the University of Lancaster.

Christine Leland works at Indiana University - Purdue University at Indianapolis in Indiana.

David Lewis is a lecturer in Education at the University of Exeter.

Alison Littlefair is an educational consultant in Cambridge.

Tony Martin works at the Lake District campus of the University of Lancaster.

Jane Medwell lectures in Education at the College of St Mark & St John, Plymouth.

Joyce Morris is an educational consultant in London.

Keith Nettle is Publishing Director of NFER-Nelson.

Pamela Owen lectures in English at S. Martins College, Lancaster.

Juliet Partridge lectures at the University of Tasmania at Launceston in Tasmania.

Lucinda Pease-Alvarez works in the School of Education, San Jose State University, California

Louise Poulson is a lecturer in Education at the University of Exeter.

Joseph D. Rivard works at Central Michigan University in Michigan.

Julie Spreadbury lectures at the Queensland University of Technology in Queensland, Australia.

Loreta Stewart works in the Division of Language and Literature at Jordanhill College, Glasgow.

Marion Tonjes is Professor of Education at Western Washington University, Washington, U.S.A.

Jo Weinberger is a researcher at the University of Sheffield.

David Wray lectures in Education at the University of Exeter.